IMAGES
of America

SAN LUIS OBISPO
COUNTY ARCHITECTURE

Madonna Inn's (in)famous urinal was memorialized by Weird Al Yankovic, then a Cal Poly architecture student, in his first release, "Take Me Down," for a 1978 San Luis Obispo (SLO) County Equal Opportunity Commission LP: If you're new in town / And you wanna look around / But you don't know where to begin, / Well, there's Bubblegum Alley / And the local car rally, / Not to mention the toilets at Madonna Inn. (Photograph by James Papp.)

ON THE COVER: Hearst Castle's pergola was defined by height and length: needing to be high enough for "a tall man with a tall hat on a tall horse," according to William Randolph Hearst, who ordered it; "the longest pergola in captivity," according to Julia Morgan, who designed it. Seen here under construction, its concrete columns and beams wind a mile around Orchard Hill, with La Cuesta Encantada, the enchanted hill, in the distance. (Photograph by J.J. Boy.)

IMAGES
of America

SAN LUIS OBISPO
COUNTY ARCHITECTURE

James Papp

ARCADIA
PUBLISHING

Copyright © 2023 by James Papp
ISBN 9781-4671-6004-9

Published by Arcadia Publishing
Charleston, South Carolina

Printed in the United States of America

Library of Congress Control Number: 2023935830

For all general information, please contact Arcadia Publishing:
Telephone 843-853-2070
Fax 843-853-0044
E-mail sales@arcadiapublishing.com

Visit us on the Internet at www.arcadiapublishing.com

In memory of four good friends: historian Alex Gough, visionary Ken Schwartz, poet Basil Jenkins, and yachtsman Konrad Huntley

CONTENTS

ACKNOWLEDGMENTS

Unless otherwise noted, all images appear courtesy of the History Center of San Luis Obispo County. The generosity of History Center executive director Thomas Kessler and the tireless assistance and understanding of collections manager Brittany Webb have made this book possible. Others who have been of great help include former History Center executive director Eva Ulz, Jessica Holada and Laura Sorvetti of Cal Poly Special Collections and Archives, Brian Leveille of the City of San Luis Obispo Community Development Department, Dan Krieger, Jean Martin, Eric Meyer, Bill Pierotti, Vicky Kastner, Eric Smith, and the yak tityu tityu yak tiłhini/Northern Chumash.

INTRODUCTION

This is a book for learning the dozens of languages of California's architecture, how they are spoken on the street, and what they mean. In a wild, beautiful place at the edge of the world, people wanted to build buildings that gave meaning as well as shelter. Far from the cultural capitals of Europe, Asia, Africa, the East Coast and Midwest, and even San Francisco and Los Angeles, San Luis Obispans wanted to be at the cutting edge of architecture. They conjured up the ancient Greeks, ancient Egyptians, Medieval Gothic, the Renaissance, Palladio, and their own invention. They used thatch, adobe, wood, corrugated iron, concrete, glass, found objects, and neon tubes. A dairy farmer or undertaker could become an architect. Outside architects could be lured here, like Julia Morgan, or design at a distance, like Frank Lloyd Wright. We could even rebel against architecture, like Warren Leopold, who so often signed himself "Not a Licensed Architect" that his family engraved it on his tombstone.

It's harder for us highbrows to snoot the Madonna Inn knowing it interweaves Heimatstil, Ranch, and National Park Service (NPS) Rustic to express Alex Madonna's Swiss Italian, cowboy, and highway engineering backgrounds; knowing its pinkness comes from Phyllis Madonna via the Mission Revival Motel Inn, borrowed from the Mission Revival Beverly Hills Hotel, from the Mission Revival Royal Hawaiian in Honolulu, and finally from the Argentine president's Neobaroque Casa Rosada in Buenos Aires. Architecture has as complicated a psychology and genealogy as people do.

It's easier for us lowbrows to have fun knowing how our environment got built, not only symbolically but physically. As someone who works in construction, I love to see how different people have solved different problems and kept their buildings warm, dry, and upright.

I hope "nobrows"—eager to tear down physical memories in the name of money and progress—may become more hesitant. Demolishing an old building kills a language, ends a story, pushes out a community, inflates the cost of housing, and heats the planet.

Listen carefully to buildings. Generations of highbrows have looked at the tile roof, stucco walls, and arched entrances of Julia Morgan's 1934 Monday Club in San Luis Obispo and called it "Mission Revival." One picture is worth a thousand words, and I'll save you reading two thousand by showing, on the next page, the Monday Club with its model, Andrea Palladio's 1549 Villa Poiana. Palladian architecture resurged in the early 20th century, as new books were published on the Italian master with photographs of his villas. San Luis Obispo County was on the cutting edge.

The poet and architecture critic John Betjeman described street buildings as "a public art gallery that is always open." The buildings here are a mix of the destroyed and preserved, which you can still experience in three dimensions. Take the grammar and vocabulary of the buildings here, and use them to listen to the stories every building tells.

Palladio's Villa Poiana (above) is seen in George Loukomski's 1927 *L'Oeuvre d'Andrea Palladio: Les Villas des Doges de Venise*. For the Monday Club (below), Julia Morgan removed the villa's upper story (used for storing grain, which the Monday Club did not have); dispensed with statues; shrunk the side entrances into sidelights; and transformed the broad, flat arch into louvres topped with a faux keystone, glazing its interior with a fanlight. She then switched the hip roof for side gables so she could repeat the entrance facade on Andrews Street—à la Palladio's four-fronted La Rotonda but with only two needed. Morgan retained Poiana's open pediment and four ground-floor flanking windows and then added the columns and beams of faux pergolas—used before at Phoebe Hearst's Hacienda del Pozo de Verona at Pleasanton and designed to be filled in with trellises and vines. (Below, photograph by James Papp.)

One

THE CHUMASH AND
THEIR COLONISTS

Painted Rock rises from Carrizo Plain's southwestern edge, with gray sandstone arms embracing a complex of paintings that commenced 3,000–4,000 years ago and were maintained until Whites devastated Chumash and Yokuts culture. The rock's uniqueness must have influenced its adoption as a sacred site: able to hold a group for ceremonies, hiding its images from a casual glance. It is accessible, but the Chumash prefer photographs of the paintings not be published.

The Chumash people inhabited the coast from Malibu through San Luis Obispo County, speaking seven languages and innumerable dialects, but accounts of their houses from European witnesses and later tribal consultants are consistent across the area and through several centuries. Europeans were impressed by the houses' shape ("like a half orange"), size (sleeping up to 60 people), and construction (of closely woven thatch). The Northern Chumash call the structure a *qnipu*. The photographs here are from the 1923 Ventura County Fair, when a group of Ventureño Chumash built a house in collaboration with John Harrington, who had recorded Chumash accounts of the building techniques. In 1916, Harrington worked with Rosario Cooper, the last native speaker of Northern Chumash, to write the words and structures of that language and record her songs by wax cylinder. Cooper was born in tiłhini, now San Luis Obispo, in 1844 when it had several hundred Chumash and only a dozen Whites. The yak tityu tityu yak tiłhini have since revived Northern Chumash as a living language based on Cooper's and Harrington's work. (Courtesy of the National Museum of the American Indian.)

When Gaspar de Portolá's 1769 expedition encountered a Chumash village in Price Canyon, diarist Fr. Juan Crespí did not describe the houses, presumably like the ones he had seen elsewhere and described as like "*una media naranja*." Encountering a "very small village" near Morro Rock, however, he noted they had no houses, so the Spaniards thought they were *volante*, or flying. They stopped flying long enough for 60 of them to visit the Spaniards and give them a pinole of toasted seeds, deliciously tasting like almonds. It was common to seal the base of thatched houses with dirt; one of Harrington's consultants said the San Luis Obispo Chumash used full dirt walls with tule (*Schoenoplectus acutus*) roof. Clearly durable, the pictured 1923 Chumash house, reported the *Ventura Daily Post*, was "still standing at Seaside Park" in 1924. (Both, courtesy of the National Museum of the American Indian.)

Spaniards were impressed by the *qnipu*; were Chumash impressed by ramadas and jacales? Father Serra likely performed his first, September 1, 1792, Mass at tiłhini (he spelled it Tihlini) under a ramada, his practice elsewhere. In 1894, this self-consciously historicist group barbecued beneath a ramada for the Southern Pacific's first arrival in San Luis. The earliest permanent structures of the Mission San Luis Obispo de Tolosa (Saint Louis, Bishop of Toulouse) were jacales, palings plastered with mud and thatched with tule; this jacal at Colorado's Mary Doyle Homestead gives the idea. Fr. Pedro Font, visiting tiłhini with De Anza's expedition in 1776, described in "Goldilocks style" the church as a jacal, the parish hall as a jacalon, huts for the converted Indians as jacalitos. He presciently noted the fire risk from tule thatch; months later, the mission burned from Yokuts flaming arrows. (Below, photograph by Arnold Thallheimer, courtesy of the Library of Congress.)

The jacales became embarrassing; in the early 1790s, the Spanish government in Mexico sent craftsmen to build proper mission buildings of adobe, brick, and stone. The Mission San Luis Obispo's porch and bell loft, photographed in the late 1860s, shows early signage: "VERE HIC EST DOMUS DEI ET PORTA COELI" (Truly this is the house of God and gate of heaven) and, for those who did not know Latin, "ONLY ONE FAITH ONE BAPTISM ONE GOD." Reverting to Latin again, it reads, "ERECTA MDCCLXXII" (actually 1792) and "REPARATA MDCCCLXVII." The photograph of the *corredor*, slightly later, shows tile stripped from the roof of the stone porch and bell loft—built 1830 after an earthquake—to relieve weight to keep them from collapsing. (Both, courtesy of the University of Southern California Libraries and California Historical Society.)

Here, by 1880, the porch and loft have been demolished, as has the *corredor* roof, to let in more light. The columns would soon follow. Part of the *convento* has been covered with a shingle roof and wood siding, eventually extending toward the end of the building. "A trivial little wooden belfry," as it was later called, held the displaced bells. For decades they had been ringing—and still ring today—a call to Mass unique to San Luis, to whose tune the bell-ringers sing, "The beans are done, the beans are done, if you don't come now you won't get none." A church fire in 1920 galvanized efforts to restore the mission to its earliest documented form with authentic adobe bricks, seen here drying in the mission yard, with Addison Chong's restaurant and Ah Louis's store in the background. (Above, courtesy of the Huntington Library.)

The stone-built Asistencia Santa Margarita de Cortona was more sophisticated than the mostly mud-built neighboring missions. Boston businessman Alfred Robinson, riding from Monterey to Santa Barbara in the early 1830s, found nothing to say about San Miguel or San Luis but waxed eloquent about the Asistencia: "On an eminence that overlooked the grounds, an extensive building was erected. It was divided into storerooms for different kinds of grain and apartments for the accommodation of the majordomo, servants, and wayfarers. At one end was a chapel, and snug lodging rooms for the priest, who, I was informed, frequently came and passed some weeks at the place during the time of harvest, and the holy friars of the two missions occasionally met there to acknowledge to each other their sins." German businessman Edward Vischer drew its ruins in 1864. The image below was photographed by John Galloway in 1882. (Below, courtesy of the University of Southern California Libraries and California Historical Society.)

After the secularization of the missions, the Asistencia became part of the Rancho Santa Margarita, granted to Joaquín Estrada while his half-brother, Juan Bautista Alvarado, was governor of Alta California. Another brother got the adjoining land grant, Rancho Asunción. Once the US Public Land Commission confirmed Estrada's ownership in 1861, he sold it to the Murphys, who also bought Rancho Asunción. The Murphys sold it to the Reises in 1904. Here, men harvest stone from the Asistencia during the Reis era around 1906. By the time the Historic American Buildings Survey (HABS) sent a photographer and researcher in a Great Depression make-work scheme, only a few walls remained. The ruins of the Asistencia, now a California State Historical Landmark and enclosed within a barn, remain on private land. (Above, courtesy of the University of Southern California Libraries and California Historical Society; below, courtesy of the Library of Congress.)

Mission San Miguel Arcángel's arcade predates the church, rebuilt in 1818 after a fire. Mission churches were generally simple, wide as obtainable beams (San Miguel's were hauled 40 miles), featuring adobe-supported beams, plank ceilings, and a low-pitched roof. Churches built in the 1810s lack accreted towers, bell gables, and Flemish-gabled false fronts of earlier missions, with enslaved Indian workforces already dissipating. San Miguel compensates with magnificent interior paintings—the only mission system murals in largely original state. Barcelona-born, Monterey-based merchant Estéban Munrás designed them, and Salinan Indians executed them. They are 2D presentations of 3D Greek Revival, with Doric columns and entablatures with alternating triglyphs and rosettes, Baroque balustrades with pinecone finials, wonky Greek key borders, tiles, hangings, and bursts of light from the Holy Spirit. (Marble-carved Doric triglyphs were wood-beam-joint skeuomorphs—stylistic references to vestigial functions, like vinyl roofs on hardtop cars.) (Above, photograph by William Henry Jackson, courtesy of the Huntington Library; below, courtesy of the University of Southern California Libraries and California Historical Society.)

Munras's 2D balustrade is juxtaposed with the choir loft's 3D. (Balusters, named for their resemblance to pomegranate blossoms [*balausta*], were invented by Donato Bramante in 1502.) In the mission's house library, Franciscan brother Albert Coucke—born 1893 in the Bay Area to Belgian parents and trained at the California School of Arts and Crafts in Oakland and California School of Fine Arts in San Francisco—painted murals depicting the early life of St. Francis, founder of the order that founded the missions (naming them for Franciscan saints). Coucke restored the Mission San Antonio de Padua's murals after World War II and then, during the early 1950s, painted his own murals at nearby San Miguel. St. Francis himself begged stones for church restoration after a vision of Jesus told him to "go and repair my house, which, you see, is in ruins." (Above, courtesy of the University of Southern California Libraries and California Historical Society; below, photograph by James Papp.)

Two

GREEK AND GOTHIC REVIVALS, ITALIANATE, AND NEOCLASSICAL

Petronillo Rios's adobe, photographed before its two 20th-century declines and two restorations, is classic Greek Revival and faces the highway with a square-columned portico, Roman lattice balustrade, central and flanking French doors, and side-gabled roof. The two-story Greek Revival adobe is often called Monterey style, though the first documented one (now demolished) was built in Santa Barbara by Capt. Alpheus Thompson of Maine (a Greek Revival hotbed) in 1834. (Courtesy of the C.C. Pierce Collection, Huntington Library.)

Straightening of newly christened US Route 101 in 1930 almost doomed the Rios-Caledonia, but the Federated Women's Clubs' History and Landmarks Section, backed by the Automobile Club, hotel association, and Chamber of Commerce, intervened, and the highway was rerouted behind the adobe. Charles Dorries restored it as a tourist attraction; 40 years later, the county acquired and re-restored the then-ruinous adobe for a museum, which it remains. Edna Valley's Leff Adobe, demolished in 1897, lacked a portico but nonetheless communicated its Greek Revival style through its plainness, symmetry, hip roof variant, and rectangular transom light above the door. In Roman-inspired Neoclassical architecture, this last would have been an arched fanlight, but the Greeks used arches only for sewers.

Immigrant Frenchman Pierre Dallidet married Asencion Zalazar, daughter of a San Luis land grantee, building a one-room Greek Revival adobe on her family's property in 1860 and founding the county wine industry in adjoining vineyards. In 1954, with the couple's youngest son Paul still living in the adobe, Boy Scout Gregory Morris photographed its square columns, Roman lattice balustrade, and rectangular transom light. Paul willed it to the County Historical Society, which preserves and keeps it open. In 1851, surveyor William Hutton drew the one-and-a-half story, side-gabled, open-porticoed Greek Revival of Francis Ziba Branch, New York–born grantee, in the late 1830s, of the 26.5-square-mile Rancho Santa Manuela, Arroyo Grande Valley. Branch was a close friend of Alpheus Thompson and shared his architectural taste. This photograph shows the conversion to two stories, a hip roof, a partial portico enclosure—and subsequent ruin.

Boston-born William Dana (rhymes with *manna*) was granted the 59-square-mile Rancho Nipomo in 1837. The one-and-a-half-story, side-gabled house was photographed for the Historic American Buildings Survey during the Great Depression. Claimed as the county's oldest house (the 1801–1810 Sauer-Adams Adobe—still inhabited—is), the Dana is the rare Greek Revival with porticos on opposing sides, plus shortened top-floor windows like New York Greek Revival townhouses, captured in 1954 by indefatigable Boy Scout Gregory Morris. A building with columns on four sides—a peripteros, like some Greek temples—was the Greek Revival ideal. Captain Thompson managed a semi-peripteral three sides. In California, only General Vallejo achieved a full peripteron on his extant Greek Revival adobe at Rancho Petaluma. The Dana Adobe has been restored as a historic house museum in its original rural setting. (Above, courtesy of the Library of Congress.)

This side-gabled, open-porticoed, board and batten Greek Revival—once western neighbor of the Mission San Luis Obispo—was the town's second house of lumber, shipped around Cape Horn by Dundee-born Capt. John Wilson and San Diego–born Ramona Carillo Pacheco Wilson. Owning hundreds of square miles throughout Alta California, in 1845, the Wilsons even bought the mission (later returned to the church by the United States). In 1904, the Carnegie Library displaced the house. To the mission's east, in this c. 1900 photograph, the Sauer-Adams Adobe contains two of the last three of 80 Indian slave adobes that once flanked Chorro Street; the Sauer Adobe is the third. Around 1860, the German Sauers added a second adobe floor to the Sauer-Adams, clad it in redwood, and, like Captain Thompson's adobe, gave it a bracket-supported, square columned gallery and door and window pediments.

Pioneer California landscape photographer Carleton Watkins took the wood frame Eagle Hotel, northwest corner of Monterey and Osos Streets, San Luis Obispo, in 1877, showing an urban Greek Revival portico in use: men below, women above, and a toddler balanced on the Roman lattice. In 1884, the Eagle was jacked up and moved a half block; in 1885, it was replaced by the Andrews Hotel, which, in 1886, burned to the ground; in 1887, the Eagle met the same fate. Camp Roberts (pictured) and Camp San Luis both got Greek Revival service clubs at the beginning of World War II. Not inconceivably, this Greek Revival revival had something to do with the 1939 hit *Gone with the Wind*. As with *Gone with the Wind*, Black soldiers were not admitted. The Camp Roberts Historical Museum operates in another Greek Revival—the World War II Red Cross headquarters. (Above, courtesy of the California State Library.)

The extraordinary Hays-Latimer Adobe, perhaps the only Gothic Revival adobe house, was probably designed and built by Irish-born civil engineer William C. Parker in the early 1860s; Edward Vischer drew it in 1864. Based on the architecture of Alexander Jackson Davis, who borrowed the Greek peripteros for Gothic and Swiss Revival styles, the Hays-Latimer shares with Davis's famous Lyndhurst a semi-peripteral portico of open-spandrel Tudor arches supported by compound columns (or the frontier equivalent: redwood two-by-sixes crossed with two-by-fours). The attic vent, referencing a Gothic quatrefoil window, is formed with an adobe corbel arch. The crow-stepped adobe gable is hidden by the redwood siding. Adobe, siding, and three-side portico were likely built simultaneously, for climate control blow and architectural show. Parker sold to Dr. W.W. Hays, an American Tree-Planting Movement enthusiast, as seen in the c. 1900 photograph. (Below, both photographs by James Papp.)

The county built its first official structure—a jail—in 1860, two years after six men were hanged before the Mission San Luis after vigilante trials. San Francisco architect Louis R. Townsend chose brick and Gothic Revival, perhaps thinking the lancet door's ecclesiastical atmosphere would induce charity, at least order. But in 1861, according to the *Sacramento Daily Union*, a Californio who had confessed to rape was being led in when a party "followed to the jail door and took him from the officer, placed him in a wagon, and drove off at full speed to about a mile below town, and hung him to the limb of a tree." The sheriff cut him down alive; the "exasperated" Californios determined a mob should not lynch him, but the next day 50 armed Americans "marched to the jail, bursted the doors open, and hung him in the jail yard doorway." In 1870, the *Tribune* opined, "A moderately long-nailed wildcat could scratch itself out of the place in half an hour." A new courthouse-jail was finished in 1873.

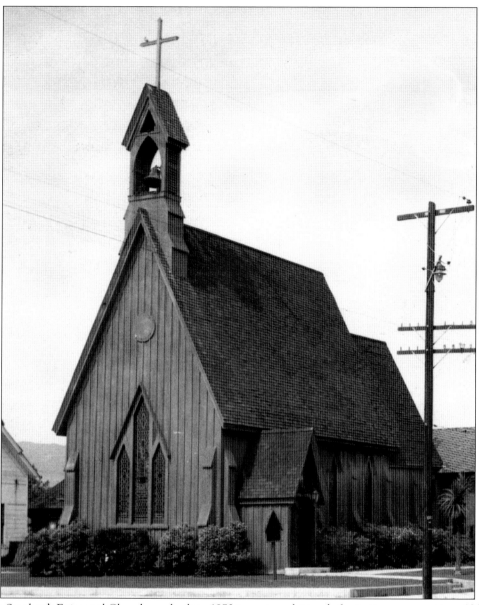

St. Stephen's Episcopal Church was built in 1873 to seat—ambitiously for its tiny congregation—100. It copies St. Michael's Longstanton, a 13th-century stone and thatch church in Cambridgeshire promoted by the Ecclesiological Society, a group founded by Cambridge undergraduates in 1839 to spread piety based on Early English church architecture. The model was elegant and economical, with a nave under a single canopy; a smaller chancel to the east; a bellcote rising, above a compound lancet window, from the west wall instead of a separate tower; and a small south porch. Stone, brick, and even clapboard versions were built in the United States and Canada in the late 1840s. British cabinetmaker Richard Upjohn, who in America became an ecclesiastical architect, seems, in 1853, to have been the first to execute it in vertical board and batten, later used across the Old West. St. Stephen's is narrower than St. Michael's, has a compound window of three rather than two lancets, couldn't manage curvature in their arches, and has two right-angle buttresses at each corner rather than one at 45 degrees but is otherwise its American cousin.

These two Gothic Revival cottages in Cambria, a mining boomtown, show the compromises of frontier style, where periodically available architectural details were imported from the east. Both have high-pitched roofs, acute-angled gables, gable finials, and Gothic Revival fretwork hanging like icicles from eaves and window canopies. The one at the top has—like the Hays-Latimer Adobe—Tudor arches with open spandrels, but the chamfered square columns with capitals and astragals (the molding near the top) are Italianate (as is the building's ell footprint). The other, dwarfed by the Neobaroque Ramage & Conway store (constructed 1875 "on the old plan of tenon and mortise," per the *Tribune*), has a more characteristically Gothic center-façade gable, but the front porch canopy is held up by Tuscan columns (from Neoclassical architecture), supporting a balustrade of Donato Bramante's balusters, then an Italianate reference.

Three American churches (two at Cypress Lawn in Colma and Forest Lawn in Glendale) claim to be based on St. Giles, Stoke Poges, where Thomas Gray is supposed to have composed *Elegy Written in a Country Churchyard*, which became the most popular English poem of the 19th century. Despite images of St. Giles being widely circulated (above), none of the three resembles the distinctive original. But San Luis Obispo's First Presbyterian Church (below) does—from the flared roof of the side aisles of the nave (viewed from the west of both churches) to the castellated tower. Los Angeles architect Thornton Fitzhugh, adept at revival styles, designed it but seems never to have mentioned St. Giles as his model. First Presbyterian was built in 1905 of local Bishop Peak granite. The magnificent interior trusswork is worth sitting through a sermon. The watercolor above is from 1910. (Above, courtesy of the Alexander Turnbull Library, New Zealand.)

Large, elaborate houses are often what historians and preservationists focus on, whether because important people lived there, the costliest architects were hired, money was lavished on construction, or the modern historic preservation movement, intended in large part to lift up decayed neighborhoods, was co-opted by the upper middle class. These two cottages, one in Santa Margarita and one at Santa Rosa Creek, embodied the Italianate style despite their modesty. Their gables were obtuse (usually in the range of 105–125 degrees for Italianate) with a wide, plain frieze below. The side-gabled cottage with a full-width porch was characteristically Italianate, as was the ell with an asymmetric porch. Both had characteristically Italianate shiplap siding and chamfered square columns, even if their means did not run to capitals or astragals. And both, house-proudly, had board and batten additions hidden in the back.

The 1877 Hathway House (demolished) and 1878 Jack House and Garden (now a public park in San Luis) have all the bells and whistles of Italianate: eave corbels and panels, window crowns, faux quoining at the corners of the Hathway, pilasters on the bay windows of the Jack, roof balustrades (the Hathway's 2D), and entrance canopies. The balustraded faux roof terrace with faux chimney atop the Jack House was intended not for widows to walk on but as a stylistic borrowing from Italian Baroque. Wood Italianate often had elaborately painted detail and often was marmoreally white, but both houses are characteristically asymmetric—more useful than symmetrical designs for accommodating later add-ons, as the practical and hugely popular contemporary architecture writer Andrew Jackson Downing, a disciple of Alexander Jackson Davis, pointed out.

Buildings outlive gardens. The Jack House is one of thousands of Italianate houses in California; its surviving Gardenesque landscape is probably unique. Influential Scottish landscape architect John Claudius Loudon disapproved of 18th-century Picturesque landscapes, with clumps of vegetation pretending to be natural. Instead, Loudon proposed isolated and highly cultivated exemplars of rare plants be set among lawns and winding paths, and he called it Gardenesque. In the 1880s, Mary Hollister Banning and Nellie Hollister Jack posed in the Jack Garden beneath a young *Washingtonia filifera*, the only native California palm, in a portrait of Nellie's garden. The detail from a c. 1880 bird's-eye view of "The celebrated El Paso de Robles hot and cold Sulphur springs" by civil engineer Edward Fairman combines two landscapes: Gardenesque winding paths and Baroque formal squares—the Old West reimagined as a spa town. (Above, courtesy of the Jack House, City of San Luis Obispo Department of Parks and Recreation.)

San Luis's Italianate Court School (constructed 1877) presaged the Jack House's rooftop balustrade, shared its squared-columned entrance with a balustraded canopy, and threw in arched windows. The district took its first mandated children's census in 1876; recorded 582 Whites, 10 Chinese, and an Indian; and promptly excluded the latter 11 from school. During World War II, the old Court School made way for the new White USO. The Black USO, first expediently placed in Chinatown, then replaced the old White USO in a Mission Revival on Higuera. A riot ensued when the neighboring bar refused Black servicemen; 200 Blacks were arrested and 200 Whites let off. The magnificently proportioned Hotel Marre, by dairyman-turned-architect Hilamon Spencer Laird, rose at the foot of the Pacific Coast Steamship pier in Port San Luis—the easiest route to the county until 1901. It closed in 1921, burning in 1934.

Neoclassicism dominated American courthouse design in the 19th century, though why Rome was thought particularly iconic of justice (alternatively, order) is not clear. The 1873 County Courthouse by San Francisco architect Thomas Johnson was not quite right. In Neoclassical architecture, round columns typically supported a pediment, whereas here square columns supported a balustraded porch like an Italianate villa. Brick was purpose-made in San Luis, concealed by stucco etched with faux ashlar (smooth stone). The ground floor lacked the usual rustication (rough cut), though its stucco was tinted, matching the pilasters, and it had round and segmental arches, while the upper floors' rectangular windows just had rounded corners. William Weeks's 1908 Paso Robles Carnegie Library has a proper Rustic (though of concrete, not stone) and brick piano nobile, with concrete faux quoining and cartouches (rectangular Roman and scrolled Renaissance). It now houses the Paso Robles History Museum.

Three

SWISS HEIMATSTIL AND STICK

Alex Madonna (left) is pictured during Madonna Inn expansion in 1962. No architecture in the county—except Hearst Castle/Xanadu—better represents psyche: Swiss Heimatstil for Alex's four Swiss Italian grandparents; Ranch for his Chorro Valley childhood, interrupted by his father's death and the family's move to San Luis; and National Park Service Rustic, incorporating the Central Coast boulders from his career building highways. The result is a unique super motel he refused to turn into a chain.

Swiss Heimatstil (homeland style), based on Alpine folk architecture, was the first of the 19th-century National Folk Revival movements, but it seems to have started in England as an exotic idiom in 1839, with Samuel Brooks's "Cottage in the Swiss Style" in *Designs for Cottage and Villa Architecture*. It moved to America in 1850 through Andrew Jackson Downing's *Cottage Residences*. Only then did it capture Central Europe. Downing's "Swiss Cottage" was a tall house with jerkinhead gables (a small hip at the gable top), deep eaves with knee brackets, and turned and fretwork decoration, like David and Carrie Meredith's 1883 hillside San Luis house. When Swiss-born Cayucos dairyman Antonio Tognazzini built his San Luis house in the 1890s, his homeland idioms of gable decoration, extended shed eaves, and wedge-roofed towers were already familiar to American contractors. The image below was photographed by L.M. Fitzhugh in 1904.

Antonio Tognazzini's daughter Clelia married banker Romilio Muscio, whose parents were also Swiss Italian immigrants, in 1898. When they could afford to build a house, they built in Heimatstil of the Chalet subtype on the 1300 block of Mill Street in San Luis Obispo's Fremont Heights. The two-dimensional fretwork balcony balusters were not an economic necessity but a Swiss specialty (Laubsägelistil, in German). The house still stands, now as the Chalet Apartments. When Alex Madonna went into construction after spending World War II in the Army Corps of Engineers, his brand of Heimatstil informed private houses in his own San Luis Drive neighborhood, as well as the Madonna Inn. This one incorporates a chalet gable, rafter tails, polygonal extensions, a cupola, and a Mid-Century Modern river rock dado. (Both photographs by James Papp.)

The mythology is that the Madonnas put up a few rooms, and then guests urged them to add amenities. In fact, Alex's super motel, an idealistic reaction to dismal highway lodging he encountered while road building, was fully planned with Beverly Hills architect Louis Gould for 160 rooms in more than a dozen buildings. This 1957 concept shows chalet gables; towers; Swiss Gothic needle spires; long, bunkhouse-like structures for the rooms; and plenty of parking. Conceived as the San Luis Inn, it opened as Madonna Inn. A bleak January 1959 view of the first, linear buildings shows them surrounded by dirt and the hill behind shrouded in fog. But the Ranch footprint and Swiss forms only wait for pavilions, spires, and boulders—and for Phyllis Madonna to apply pink paint and create the panoply of theme guest rooms.

As the Madonnas expanded, they improvised, adding a Ranch-length, Swiss-form porte cochère with alternate shed- and gable-roofed oriel windows—fretworked (Laubsägelistil) and half-timbered (Fachwerkstil)—atop mounds of NPS Rustic boulders. (From the turn of the century, National Park Service lodges had combined Chalet style with Adirondack-style logs and boulders.) Initially, Madonna Inn buildings were painted buff. San Luis Obispo's Mission Revival Motel Inn had gone pink, however, emulating the Mission Revival Beverly Hills Hotel and Royal Hawaiian. Pink was also Motel Inn owner Marge Calkins' favorite color. When her friend Phyllis borrowed it for the Madonna Inn, she transformed rustic to *la vie en rose*. Melding Hollywood sophistication to Alex's Swiss-Ranch-Rustic, Phyllis also began to decorate each room individually and outrageously. Here, she takes charge of the kitchen. Naturally, Copper Café tabletops are from Alex's own mine.

Madonna Inn, a California icon handcrafted between 1959 and 1969 in wood, wrought iron, stone, and stained glass, is the Watts Tower of comfort, Nitt Witt Ridge of commercialism, Hearst Castle of the middle class—also the apotheosis of Motelism, the simultaneous streamlining and valorization of transience. A few years earlier, exiled Russian aristocrat Vladimir Nabokov became obsessed with American motels, using them for the road trip of his 1955 picaresque *Lolita*, where Humbert Humbert's Old World sophistication runs smack into Dolores Haze's adolescent Americanness. "The Pale Palace of the Enchanted Hunters" is a prevision of Madonna Inn: the arclights, "row of parked cars, like pigs at a trough," "maudlin murals depicting enchanted hunters," and "overstuffed blood-red armchair." "'Wow! Looks swank,' remarked my vulgar darling squinting at the stucco as she crept out into the audible drizzle." Vladimir Nabokov and Alex Madonna both captured the zeitgeist—Nabokov called it пóшлость—of midcentury America, and the works of both endure. When Madonna died, he was borne in a horse-drawn hearse through streets draped and crowds dressed in pink instead of mourning. (Photograph by James Papp.)

The great architectural historian Vincent Scully considered Andrew Jackson Downing's 1850 "Swiss Cottage"—which the Meredith House (seen page 36) is based on—to be the ur-house of what Scully christened, a century later, Stick style. It represented to him the willingness of the American architectural establishment to countenance lumber as a respectable material, with exterior wood decoration referencing the structure within. Swiss folk architecture does extend its structure to the outside in beam ends, rafter tails, and half-timber (timber frame structure filled in with plaster). Downing glibly distilled these to surface decoration, and a style developed that was less overtly Swiss but still used slats, fretwork, finials, and lobed and perforated bargeboards (like the Roselip House in Edna Valley), and knee brackets and board and batten (like this unidentified local house and water tower).

Stick turned up in railroad stations, perhaps because passengers needed to huddle under deep eaves. A bad habit of people writing architectural history is dismissing what they cannot figure out as "vernacular," that is, local, functional, of no style (like Gloria Grahame in *The Big Heat* responding to Glenn Ford's Colonial Revival hideout with "Say, I like this: early nothing!"). "Railroad Vernacular" has been stamped on many Stick structures, but Templeton's 1888 station had ogee knee brackets and a gable finial at one end and a hip roof tower with second-floor battens at the other. Oceano's 1896 station has lobed bargeboards and combines wall shingle, novelty siding, and shiplap from top to bottom. The rectangular bays and the vertical plank trim that Scully found iconic on Downing's Swiss Cottage feature (or featured) in both. Oceano Depot, now a museum, is well worth the visit.

In the Old West, no building more than the schoolhouse was built as its community's flagship, and no building was more quickly demolished for "progress." This one, costing $5,000, rose spectacularly from the Nipomo plains in 1888, with a lightning rod, bell tower tent-roofed with corbelled shed extensions and columns, slat trim moved forward to hang from the lobed bargeboards, horizontal bands of slats and fishscale shingle, more corbelled shed canopies over first-floor doors and windows, and ingenious right-angle stairs. Nipomo's school census that year revealed 166 children between 5 and 17, 119 of whom had attended school the previous year, 47 of whom had not; perhaps the school was designed to attract the latter. Nipomo's name comes from the Rancho Nipomo, the 1837 Dana land grant, which got its name from Chumash *nipumuʔ*, the place of the big house.

Hilamon Spencer Laird, the designer of the 16th Agricultural District Pavilion, was not the first pure architect—rather than builder-architect—in San Luis. He was the first who stayed, however, practicing for four decades. His 1887 pavilion accommodated district fairs and subsequently a women's club and theater—though losing the top of its extraordinary oriel tower, supported by huge knee brackets and open framework (partly visible behind 1909 elephant leg columns). The side entrance on Toro had a wide chalet gable. The main entrance had vertical and horizontal board and shingle panels separated by plank trim, faux half-timbering, shed canopies, and even segmental arches and oculus windows (these last having nothing to do with Stick but stylish nonetheless). Its former site is now a parking lot, but at least 10 Laird buildings survive elsewhere in San Luis.

Light House at Port San Luis, Cal.

The 1890 Point San Luis Lighthouse—now beautifully restored among dramatic coastal views—employs chalet references like ogee-carved bargeboards and slat gable decoration (descending from the roof gable's bargeboard and attached to the wall of the rectangular bay). Knee brackets, corbels, and molded beam ends support porches, eaves, and the tower gallery. That the lighthouse is square board and batten rather than round is a Stick feature; Point Fermin Lighthouse, San Pedro is similar, 16 years earlier. Paso Robles's 1888, $25,000 hot sulfur spring bathhouse also had characteristic square Stick towers; their tent roofs were refined with flared eaves and finialed faux half-timbered dormers. Vertical boards topped by corbels give Stick definition to the towers and semi-octagonal pavilion, glazed at ground and clerestory levels. Inside were 32 private, electrically lit, steam-heated bathing rooms and a communal tepid pool.

Featuring a square tower with flared tent roof and modillions (flat horizontal brackets), lobed bargeboards, and square bay window and without knee brackets, gable trim, or vertical wood boards (except corner boards), the McManus House, across from St. Stephen's Episcopal Church at Nipomo and Pismo in San Luis Obispo, is a late, streamlined version of Stick, more focused on shape than trim. One might call it "Stickless Stick." For so dramatic a house, its origin is unclear; it was built sometime around the late 1890s. The modern use as a group home gave it an inelegant addition, but it still stands and communicates the significance of its architectural style. Its porch's Chinese Chippendale–like balustrade and openwork frieze are characteristically Stick. (Photograph by James Papp.)

Four

CLOTH, WOOD, IRON, BRICK, AND CONCRETE

The tent has a long history in American life, from Plains Indians to armies, work parties, migrants, vacationers, homeless, and glampers. In March 1936, two days after Dorothea Lange photographed a forlorn labor camp outside Nipomo—where families had been waiting weeks for the spring pea harvest—her *Migrant Mother* images appeared in the *San Francisco News*, causing the federal government to rush aid to the destitute families. (Courtesy of the Library of Congress.)

Tent City Pizmo, Cal.

In the Old West, cities often started as tents, progressing to log cabins, box frames, balloon frames, and, finally, masonry. So severe were the shortages of materials and skilled labor during the California Gold Rush that interior and even exterior house walls often consisted of muslin: a resident in one wrote that a housebreaker would need only a pair of scissors. Tent cities for summer vacations, however, date to the 1890s; Pismo's dated to 1905, with two blocks of 14-by-18-foot four-room tents boasting wood floors, furnishings, electricity, gas heaters, water, sewerage, laundry service, garbage collection—and no liquor sold on the premises. In an era when people thought disease was passed by miasma rather than germs, tent living was the cure.

The Attractive Interior of in Tent City Pizmo Beach, Cal

Campers and glampers used wall tents. The army used bell tents, including, during the Civil War, the Sibley tent, patented in 1856 by Capt. Henry Hopkins Sibley. His patented improvements—such as smoke cowls and perimeter tent pegs instead of guy ropes—were taken from Plains Indians, who did not earn a royalty. Sibley did, until joining the Confederacy. Tents for 1908 army maneuvers at Atascadero combined bell and wall, with the walls drawn up for ventilation. An early World War II postcard by "Lennie" of the Chorro Valley's Camp San Luis shows over 1,000 rectangular wall tents. Here, Lennie photographed tar paper barracks during the transition to wood. The Japanese American families shipped from their Chorro Valley farmhouses to high desert concentration camps (as the government and press called them) also were packed in tar paper barracks but never saw them upgraded.

Established builders had little incentive to "light out for the Territory," in Huck Finn's words, so ingenuity invented a form the less skilled could construct. Traditional timber frames—mortise and tenon joints connecting heavy posts and beams—found a replacement in 1832 Chicago with the balloon frame: milled two-by-fours hammered together with machine-made nails. It remains the basis for today's suburban construction. Neighboring balloon frames designed by architect William Weeks for merchant Jacob Crocker and head clerk J.C. Naylor went up on San Luis's Nob Hill at Buchon and Chorro in 1902 and survive today. Octagon houses had a mid-1800s vogue for the efficiency of materials enclosing space. The 1897 dodecagonal tabernacle at Arroyo Grande's Methodist Episcopal Encampment was even more efficient, seating 800. It was built in a month, including a one-day shingling bee with 20 volunteers. It also survives.

Even balloon frames could be too demanding for Western expansion. Enter box frames, supported by inch-thick, old-growth vertical boards; sealed by battens; and bound by two-by-fours top and bottom. They were usually one-story but often two. All box frames are board and batten, but board and batten could also be used on timber frames and balloon frames for aesthetics (see the Gothic Revival St. Stephens on page 27) or economy. This one-room schoolhouse in See Canyon or Irish Hills held up a shiplap façade, with Italianate gable and porch of square columns and fretwork corbels, to conceal a board and batten rear. In contrast, the gold miners of La Panza proudly emphasized the boards and battens of their one-room schoolhouse with a contrasting paint job.

Box frame is difficult to confirm without breaking into walls. Probably all three board and batten structures undermined next to Bridge Street's stone Oddfellows' Hall during the 1905 Arroyo Grande flood are box frames; only the collapsing one on the left shows telltale two-by-fours at the top and bottom. Box frames are surprisingly resilient. Many from the 1860s onward still survive here, with the wing additions to the Simmler Adobe at 466 Dana Street in San Luis probably the oldest. Those are covered by horizontal shiplap, a common addition, whether for looks or stabilization. Garbageman-artist Art Beal—"Captain Nitt Witt"—used board and batten for his bricolage Nitt Witt Ridge in Cambria in the mid-20th century. Contemporaneously, Cliff May was reviving board and batten for high-end suburban Ranch-style houses and and Los Angeles modernist Richard Neutra for low-end Cal Poly Depression buildings (see page 118).

Creston's tiny 19th-century jail embodied stacked-plank construction. These two-inch-thick planks of varying widths would have been fastened together; otherwise, escape would have been a literal pushover. Stacked structures tend to be simplistic but time-consuming. Part of the appeal of the adobe revival during the mid-20th century was that anyone could make adobe bricks out of the surrounding earth and then stack them up. Making and stacking them, however, was many times slower than modern construction. Equally, the iconic log cabin required only an axe and stick-to-itiveness, but stacked-log construction was not very efficient. This cottage court at the 1928 Cambria Pines Lodge conjures all the nostalgia of the log cabin without the sweat.

Henry Robinson Palmer invented corrugated iron in 1829 to roof warehouses on London's Eastern Dock. Arched perpendicular to its corrugations, it self-supported, covering large spans: "the lightest and strongest roof (for its weight) since the days of Adam," enthused the *Register of Arts and Sciences*. Hundreds, perhaps thousands, of iron kit buildings, from cabins to warehouses, shipped to the California Gold Rush from Great Britain and New York. They quickly vanished—Californians thought them ugly—and the industry switched to supplying the Antipodes, where the buildings persist. Corrugated iron resurged in the 1880s for fireproofing light industrial and entertainment structures, though firemen could not break through the roofs. The 1906 Pizmo Pavilion, a corrugated iron–roofed dance hall, burned in 1945. The next renaissance was Nissen and Quonset huts in World Wars I and II, here adapted for Sandercock moving and storage.

Ubiquitous in the Old West (and, later, Hollywood Westerns), Western False Front Commercial mimicked flat-roof masonry commercial buildings with rectangular façades on front-gabled buildings. Common by 1850, they communicated respectability. A doctor might have a peaked-roof house with a false front office next door. This view of Western False Front buildings on Higuera Street, San Luis, shows shiplap siding with Baroque Revival columns, corbels, and cornices in front and board and batten in back (and a tent to the side). The false front of the Morro Bay Post Office established its bona fides among front-gabled houses. Western False Front corner groceries were built in San Luis as late as the 1920s, including the current Del Monte Café and High Street Deli. By the 1930s, Hollywood Westerns had adopted historic rather than contemporary plots and claimed false fronts for the past.

This Oceano garage was a nice combination of Western False Front and corrugated iron (of which it was not ashamed, using it all over). The stepped façade adapting to the roof pitch is not unusual. The interior wood structure peeks through the eaves at the right. While the Western False Front of a frontier main street could be replaced imperceptibly by masonry buildings as commercial wealth grew, many false fronts were built in splendid isolation. The transition to masonry required local brickyards. This photograph from the Ah Louis (Wong) family papers is presumably in Ah Louis's brickyard, opposite the Anholm dairy farm, later the White-only Anholm development of San Luis Obispo. It shows the mixing of a clay, sand, and water batter; forming of the ball to push in the mold; sun-drying of bricks; and a kiln for burning at right. (Below, courtesy of Special Collections and Archives, Cal Poly San Luis Obispo.)

By the 1940s, bricks for San Luis buildings as early as the 1873 county courthouse were being attributed to Ah Louis (Wong On), but the first mention of his bricks in the contemporary press is 1899, with 200,000 for Hilamon Laird's Johnson Block, Chorro and Higuera Streets. When Ah Louis contracted Alfred Walker to build his store and family apartment in 1885, the surprised *Tribune* mocked his "ambition to be very much like the 'Melicanman' therefore he must have brick buildings alle same other merchants." (Ah Louis did not speak pidgin; White journalists were adept at it.) The resulting Neobaroque—pedestaled finials, geometric cornice and window crowns, and acanthine wrought iron—survives, owned by great-grandson Dr. Bill Watson. These 1886 ruins of the wood Andrews Hotel, with the brick shell of the Bank of San Luis Obispo surviving for rebuilding, show Ah Louis's prescience.

Flour is highly flammable, and San Miguel's flour mill (managed by C.A. Miller) used brick to house the engine, corrugated iron for the stack of rolls and sifters, and wood for the warehouse. The warehouse and company survive. In 1940, San Miguel acquired a phony windmill. It was built in the Netherlands, shipped to the 1939 Golden Gate International Exposition's Dutch Pavilion for a pastry shop and then brought by train south. Serially a bar, commercial garage, house, and storage unit, it survived to the 1970s. The next fireproof advance after corrugated iron and brick with cast-iron structure was poured concrete. But when lightning struck the (unfortunately wood-roofed) concrete tanks of San Luis Obispo's 1910 tank farm in 1926, six million barrels of oil exploded, burned, and spilled for five days, creating a river of fire to the sea.

Weber-Duller Co. of L.A. Constructing 1,000,000 Bbl. Concrete Reservoir at Tank Farm near San Luis Obispo, Cal. Sept. 6, 1910. Aston-Photo-no. 83

Five

NEOBAROQUE, EASTLAKE, AND RICHARDSONIAN ROMANESQUE

In the mid-19th century, architects took inspiration from the Baroque: Renaissance Neoclassicism's audacious, curvaceous descendant. Segmental pediments topped Hilamon Laird's 1877 Bank of San Luis Obispo, echoing first-floor segmental (less-than-180-degree) arches. The 1875 Schwartz (later Loobliner) Building's triangular pediment topped an attic panel flanked by scrolls. The bank's clustered Corinthian columns and convex mansard roof edge, and Schwartz's quoins and window festoons lent drama and sophistication to dirt San Luis streets.

Italianate architecture borrowed some Baroque characteristics, like rooftop balustrades, but Italianate was mainly residential architecture. Neobaroque was mainly commercial and institutional. Technology helped. Cast-iron columns and arches made Baroque detail economical, and cast-plate glass flooded businesses with light. Both were employed to build the now-demolished Schwartz-Loobliner Building and Bank of San Luis Obispo and nearby extant 1884 Sinsheimer Store, all Neobaroque. (A three-story semi-replica of the Schwartz-Loobliner was built on the same site.) But Neobaroque transcended materials, as the wood William Lyons drugstore and brick Swiss-American Supply Company (both in Cambria) attest, with their pediment-topped attic panels flanked by pedestals (and in Lyons's case finials). Lyons's pediment doubles as the peak of the roof, a frequent Western False Front feature.

Neobaroque grocery stores with covered boardwalks lined Templeton's Main Street in the early 1900s ("Groceries & Furniture" prefiguring Target and Walmart). All had roof peak–incorporating pediments. The nearest had rare sidewalls to its false front. The sidewalls seem unlikely to have obscured the roof, given the buildings were spaced, but added three-dimensionality. Neobaroque's subtypes included Second Empire, the propagandistic French Baroque architecture of Napoleon III that featured mansard roofs. The mansard efficiently doubled as a roof and extra story, both for Parisian garrets and the Lehman Ranch House near Cambria. Charles Addams did in the reputation of Second Empire mansions by housing the Addams Family in one from the 1940s. Addams's friend Alfred Hitchcock drove the nail in the coffin with Norman Bates's Second Empire house in *Psycho*.

San Luis Obispo's 1878 Second Empire city hall (and firehouse and jail) boasted, from top to bottom, a lightning rod, urn-finialed balustrade, oculus-dormered mansard, corbels, columned and faux-keystone arches with outline molding, urn-finialed cornice, more corbels, varied corner quoining and window quoining (all faux from stucco), round-arched windows paired within further arches, and segmental-arched doors with more quoining. Its builder-architect was William Rodgers, who appears to have been the local undertaker (a business certainly requiring carpentry; he later sold his undertaking business to C.H. Wever, another builder-undertaker). In 1949, the city sold city hall, derided as "ancient," possibly because of the Addams influence, though the postwar era was self-importantly "modern" and demolished or stuccoed over 19th- and early-20th-century architecture with abandon. After four years as a storage facility, it was pulled down by Joseph M. Ries, "a used merchandise dealer known as 'Second-Hand Joe.'" All that remains is the old city jail, incorporated as a storeroom at the rear of the new building, a pedestrian one-story stucco shop that was Charles Shoes for nearly 70 years.

This rare Neobaroque house on the 1400 block of San Luis Obispo's Nipomo Street, happily extant, has a stepped attic panel, dentiled cornice, and unusual dual-shaft columns. The 1980s image is by J. Barron Wiley, a professor of audio-visual education at Cal Poly, who was an indefatigable photographer of local buildings ancient and modern, monumental and mundane, the Eugène Atget of San Luis. He donated well over a thousand of his photographs to the History Center of San Luis Obispo County. The Tognini and Ghezzi general store at Cayucos was late Neobaroque, stripped down but for the roof balustrade, modillioned cornice, and attic panel stating the building's name and flanking pedestals, its date. Achille Tognini sold out of the partnership to become a contractor and then spent years and his savings trying to develop a wave turbine at Cayucos to generate electric power.

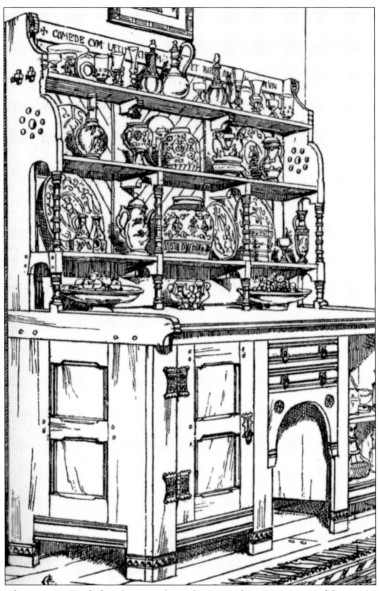

Richard Upjohn was an English cabinetmaker who moved to America and became an architect. Charles Eastlake was a trained English architect who designed cabinets. These latter birthed an eponymous American architecture. Eastlake wished to make furniture that looked as if it was from the Middle Ages—"Early English." As seen in this sideboard design from his 1868 bestseller *Hints on Household Taste*, it involved a flattened and angular form containing arches, spindles, perforations, rosettes or rondels, dogtooth molding, and emphasized joints. Other pieces used bosses, incising, and sunbursts. Americans found this easy to reproduce mechanically, compared to contemporary, more three-dimensional Renaissance and Rococo Revival furniture. Then cabinets were copied for houses, with their aesthetic suited for wood, the Western United States' dominant building material. Eastlake architecture confuses modern observers. It is frequently mistaken for Queen Anne, often reclassified as Stick-Eastlake, and not even mentioned in Virginia and Lee McAlester's *A Field Guide to American Houses*, the preservationist bible. Nonetheless, Eastlake is one of the great styles of the Old West.

The arches (and spindle-filled mini arches) of San Luis Obispo's Cortesi House (demolished) immediately indicate Eastlake. Add repetitive use of bosses (or pellet molding) on the frieze, plus square panes around the perimeters of the front windows, incised columns, perforated porch balustrade, and the filling in of wall space with shingles. The Moore House of Arroyo Grande also had perimeter panes on its offset flat and oriel windows, spindles and knobs around the entry arch, spindle columns, an array of gable surfaces, concave and convex sunbursts in the square bay corner brackets, and wood ridge cresting. One could imagine it shrunk, as a piece of furniture, in an Eastlake drawing room.

The 1890 Pitkin-Conrow House survives gloriously at 789 Valley Road in a southern extrusion of Arroyo Grande, rising like a sentinel from the alluvial vegetable fields and squat suburban subdivision opposite Halcyon. The wedge-roofed square tower is borrowed from Stick (along with surrounding finials and gable decorations), but the spindles, sunbursts, window-frame bosses, square-paned stained-glass windows, dog-tooth molding, dentillation, spindle columns, and filling of the wall surface with strips of mansard-like shingling and other patterns is all unmistakably Eastlake.

SANATORIUM.

In 1888, the *Tribune* attributed Coffee Rice's planned house to an unnamed San Diego architect (perhaps the architect, also unknown, of San Diego's similar 1887 Britt-Scripps House). Rice, a speculator in Oceano real estate, framed but left unfinished the third story. The octagonal tower is characteristically Colonial Revival but with a Châteauesque candle-snuffer roof. The arched tower windows and balcony are Eastlake, as are the lines, at the eaves, of modillions with matching rondels, with the latter unusually boxed with molding, like the perimeter border of panes in an Eastlake window. The festoons draped over the rectangular windows are Neobaroque, but there's no hint of Queen Anne. (The Britt-Scripps combines Queen Anne, Colonial Revival, and Eastlake with a three-story candle-snuffer tower.) This photograph shows the Coffee Rice in the early 1900s, while it was the Halcyon Theosophists' experimental sanatorium, exploring sound waves among other therapies. The Halcyonites finished the third story. California gardens were famed for their ability to grow plants from around the world, including, here, a three-story agave that rivals the tower.

This side view of the extant Coffee Rice House, fallen on hard times, shows modillions and rondels carried around. A first-floor faux mansard strip, like the Pitkin-Conrow's, sports more modillions. A tide of mobile homes laps against the house, once a gateway to the Oceano Dunes. In 1917, Halcyon poet John Varian and composer Henry Cowell premiered an Irish mythic pageant in the grounds, lit by colored-cellophane-covered auto headlamps—"rather queer music, a piano out of doors, played boldly and freely," with palms and forearms in tone clusters. Cowell's overture, "The Tides of Manaunaun," was later played at the White House for FDR and JFK. The extant Eastlake cottage below is San Luis Obispo's 1880s Dana-Barneberg House on Dana Street, with ridge cresting, shingled central front-facing gable, obsessive perforated drop rondels, and spindle-cornered square bays.

Eastlake was also used for institutional buildings, like the c. 1890 Creston School. Modillions, bas relief squares, wall shingles and patterning, scallops, rondels, sunbursts, and arched attic vent were all Eastlake—though a bit of Stick crept in with the shed canopies and lobed bargeboards. The house below, once on the Cuesta Grade and photographed Thanksgiving 1912, was pure Eastlake: ridge cresting; modillions; filling of gables (and bargeboards) with shingles, squares, and rondels; window perimeter panes; a border of pellet molding between first and second story; spindle columns; spindled entry canopy; and porch frieze. Perforated arch spandrels and balustrades and lobed bargeboards might recall Stick, but the former are mechanistic rather than recalling an Alpine craftsman, with the latter incised geometrically.

The 1891 First National Bank of San Luis Obispo, later the County Bank of San Luis Obispo, followed by the Commercial Bank, and now retail, is Richardsonian Romanesque for its muscular round arches, but its obsessive filling of surfaces is Eastlake-influenced. The fanlight comprises (awkwardly) Eastlake square panes, rondels cover the Gothic parapet gables (topped with foliate finials), and squares cover the spandrels of the main façade arch. East Coast architect Henry Hobson Richardson, admired today for forceful designs in rusticated stone, could also be fussy about surfaces and juxtapose Gothic with Romanesque. The First National Bank was designed by Hilamon Spencer Laird, the Point Reyes dairyman and pioneer San Luis architect, who showed knowledge of the details of Richardson's work. Like Philadelphia architect Frank Furness, Laird merged Eastlake into Gothic and Romanesque. Eastlake's furniture designs had, after all, been trying to channel the Medieval, though exuberant American Eastlake houses lost sight of that.

Time has mocked the First National Bank, shorn of gables, finials, and bellcast wedge-roofed tower long before the Santa Barbara and Long Beach earthquakes, probably more for aesthetics than seismic practicality. Stucco has covered the glorious "Eastlakery" for offending the mid-20th-century eye, leaving a few cast-iron and brick columns exposed. The skin may come off one day, but it looks like a lot of brickwork had already been bashed off. Time leaves unconquered, however, the locally quarried volcanic tuff face of W.P. Carmen's Richardsonian Romanesque building in Arroyo Grande (constructed 1904). Referred to as Caen stone for resembling the yellow limestone of northwestern France, which was used in Medieval French abbeys and English cathedrals, Los Berros stone was marketed around the state and used in an arch for the California exhibition at the 1904 St. Louis World's Fair. (Below, photograph by James Papp.)

Laird also designed the extant Andrews Bank–City Library in 1893, where the Andrews Hotel burned. A pedimented Neobaroque attic panel, flanked by Eastlake sunbursts and surrounded by massive Neobaroque ball finials, dominates the roof, descending to a Medieval arcade, its arches— round (on Monterey Street) and segmental (on Osos)—supported by quarter-round, smooth-brick engaged columns, plus two half-round, rusticated brick ones (below right) on Monterey, all with Romanesque foliate capitals. The first floor has a banded square corner column with Composite capital and banded square pilasters along the side, with a huge, muscularly framed Richardsonian arched window on square pilasters in front. Rusticated brick faces the basement, and acanthine patterns curl in spandrels and capitals. Six "Green Man" heads also peer from capitals (below left). These foliate heads, often used in Medieval churches, were revived in the late 1900s.

San Luis's 1905 Carnegie Library has two Green Men in its gables, of yellow-tinted cement to match the Los Berros tuff. William Weeks, the most prolific architect of California Carnegie libraries (22, of which 18 survive) designed the Richardsonian Romanesque building. (Laird would design the later open porch.) Bishop Peak granite was used to face the rustic—just in time, as the quarry ceased production with the death of its owner, Dr. G.B. Nichols, a month before the library opened. Los Berros tuff forms the arches, quoining, and lintels. Andrew Carnegie required plentiful ventilation and steps for people to mount to knowledge, but the most important innovation, in 1897, was self-service stacks, two decades before Piggly Wiggly patented the self-service grocery. Ionic columns and plaster festoons define the cruciform Neoclassical interior. The building, and these chairs and tables, are still in use by the county's History Center.

Not all Romanesque was Richardsonian. Henry Hobson Richardson, the second American architect educated at Paris's Ecole des Beaux-Arts, created a style that, at its best, combined elegance, gravitas, and toughness with European cultural reference—the American upper-middle-class ideal. Richardsonian Romanesque became the go-to for churches, libraries, banks, and universities. The 1875 Piedras Blancas Lighthouse is extant, but because of earthquake damage, its top has been lopped. Without the asymmetry, exaggeration, and juxtaposition of rhythms and rhythmic energy with calm emptiness that Richardson exemplified, it is an ingenious tower nonetheless, with its castle corbelling bordering top and bottom, arrow slit–like windows tucked in the faux machicolation gaps (from which boiling oil might be poured) between the upper corbels, and two curious windows on each side, with Romanesque interior and Gothic exterior arch.

San Luis Obispo's originally Baptist (now Adventist) church (constructed 1907–1908) might be called Carpenter Romanesque, like Carpenter Gothic, if wood had lent itself to round arches as it did to lancets. (Two boards could be bent into a Gothic Point; the round arches in the Baptist church require five to six bent boards. Perhaps consequently, there are scarcely any wood Romanesque churches in North America.) Los Angeles architect C.M. Brown designed it, carpenter-contractor James Akin built it, and the tower and façade of the 12th-century Eglise Saint-Hilaire de Melle inspired it—a weightless imitation. The trackside Channel Commercial wholesale grocer in San Luis, on the other hand, built as the Schwartz-Beebee warehouse around 1905 but almost immediately sold "at a sacrifice," projects heavy permanence as a battlemented castle. Adaptively reused, the pentagonal building has been defiantly rechristened Railroad Square.

The 1891 First National Bank was Hilamon Laird's first building at Chorro and Higuera Streets, the 1900 Johnson Block his second, and the 1904 Warden Junior Block his third, with the two latter occasioned by fires of multiple wood buildings grandfathered into San Luis's 1890 Fireproof Building District. The Johnson Block, the first documented building of Ah Louis bricks, is brilliant practically and aesthetically. Its cast iron structure, brick walls separating shops, and pressed brick protecting the curtain walls rode out the 1903 fire opposite. It also references the defensive curtain walls of Tuscan fortresses, with castellated office tower and shop wings. Terra-cotta bases, capitals, and astragals define brick uprights as Tuscan columns. It was ripe for obliteration with white stucco, but from 1980 to the 2010s, the stucco was removed, and the battlements were restored. With a recently proposed demolition of one wing beaten back, it endures.

Arroyo Grande's 1902 Oddfellows Hall, now a performance space for the South County Historical Society, is a Tuscan tower of Los Berros tuff. With segmental arches and subtle 2D reference to corbels and machicolation below the battlements, it was designed by lodge member A.F. Parsons, who the same year won office as county surveyor—having started 25 years before as the Las Tablas schoolteacher. In North County, the Southern Pacific (SP) reached Santa Margarita, 18 miles past Templeton, in January 1889. Whoever designed the depot was familiar with Frank Furness's 125 buildings for the Philadelphia & Reading Railroad (P&R), from 1878 to 1884, where he reworked Stick by curving rooflines and brackets, extending eaves and shed canopies, multiplying windowpanes, cantilevering brickwork, and adding wall shingles and prow-ended ridge cresting—essentially "Eastlaking" it. (Above, photograph by James Papp.)

Hilamon Laird's 1894 Shipsey House at Johnson Avenue and Mill Street in San Luis looks Furnessian, giving drama to Eastlake by rising from wings to the core, adding multilevel counterpoint to triplet windows, and defining the roof with prowed, castellated wood ridge cresting (the only San Luis building to have retained it). Castellation looked more castle-like lining the town's second Masonic Hall, built in 1875 (the 1913 fourth survives in Masonic use). Architecture was credited to contractors Lincoln, Wearmouth & Co., and Laird was then their house architect. With a pyramid of conjoined arched windows, the central one Diocletian (repeated on the side atop a three-story pyramid of windows), and with front pellet molding echoed by large rondels on the base, this accomplished building rose before Furness's forceful juxtapositions attained fame. Had Laird had a larger canvas than San Luis, America might now be talking of Lairdian architecture.

Six

QUEEN ANNE, COLONIAL REVIVAL, SHINGLE, AND FIRST BAY TRADITION

Henry Hobson Richardson not only invented Richardsonian Romanesque, but he also introduced Queen Anne Revival to America and was a founder of the Shingle style and among the earliest Colonial Revivalists. Shingle, in the Bay Area, spawned the First Bay Tradition. The 1905 beachfront Pismo Inn combined elements of Colonial Revival (the oriel-windowed tower), Shingle (natural wood sheathing), and First Bay (pagoda-like tower roof and wave-form board balustrade).

"Queen Anne" is misused of so many American architectural styles, it has become as useless a term as "Victorian" (in a country Victoria never ruled). In the 1860s, English architect Norman Shaw introduced a Jacobethan (Jacobean-Elizabethan) revival style, "which presently became known as 'Queen Anne,' for no good reason," as an American obituarist wrote. Shaw's was a big-windowed, red-brick-and-tile reaction to cold stone Gothic Revival. Richardson adopted the Elizabethan part (half-timbering, jettied [projecting] upper floors, expansive leaded windows, and large and low rooms), replacing tile-hung exterior walls with American natural wood shingles. Two San Luis Obispo buildings, the fire-razed 1885 Andrews Hotel and extant c. 1893 Biddle House on Emerson Park are "Queen Anne"—being Tudor. Sash windows, less authentic than leaded casements, are, alas, more practical. The Biddle sashes' blue-stained-glass perimeters borrow Eastlake.

PASO ROBLES SCHOOL OF MUSIC
JOHN J. ACKSON DIRECTOR

Colonial Revival, like Eastlake, is often misidentified as Queen Anne, unfortunately, since it had a huge role as America's national revival architecture in an era when Europe was reviving its own folk architecture. Colonial Revival also served as America's streamline style when European National Folk Revival was being streamlined into Jugendstil–Art Nouveau. New York's McKim, Mead, and White invented Colonial Revival around the American Centennial. Common signs of Colonial Revival houses are gables like classical pediments; a blank perimeter frieze below the eaves; canted (three sides of an octagon) or semi-circular bay windows; an octagonal or circular tower; rectangular, round, or oval accent windows or vents; and entry porch (usually asymmetrically placed) with Tuscan or occasionally Ionic columns. Some of these (like the bays and towers) reference post-Revolution Federal architecture around 1800. The 1888 Daniel and Cecelia Blackburn House, later Paso Robles School of Music, sported pediment gables, frieze, canted bays, an octagonal tower, accent windows and vents, and a porch with Tuscan columns. The Colonial Revival Crocker House (see page 50) has an octagonal lantern above its porch à la Mount Vernon.

The 1905 Stanton House, Buchon, and Garden, San Luis is notable for Edward Stanton's having embezzled $14,433.74 from his employer (the Pacific Coast Railway) to build it, besides stealing materials from the railway's yard. (Stanton was sent to San Quentin. Two years earlier, a block away, J.C. Naylor [see page 50] was found to have embezzled to build his house but on a smaller scale and self-exiled to Bakersfield.) Stanton's architect, W.C. Phillips, started his career in Arroyo Grande, moved to San Luis, and then graduated to San Jose. The round tower with curved glass and Art Nouveau fascia on the pediment gables are Colonial rarities. Like the Stanton House across the street, the 1908 Kaiser House has a curved, wraparound porch with Tuscan columns and shingle parapet. For further streamlining, it eschews gables and a tower, employing a *japoniste* bellcast roof. (Above, photograph by J. Barron Wiley.)

Hip roof Colonial Revivals, presenting their narrow end to the street, took on the look of a *hogyo* (pagoda roof) when curved. The geometric 1907 Brecheen bungalow on Pismo Street's 1100 block (extant) emphasizes the *hogyo* with the lowest pitch and deepest eaves of any San Luis Colonial. The usual front canted bay window is pressed flush, with its flanking windows half the width of its central one and muntined top panes half the height of the lower plate glass. The porch window repeats the central window's dimensions, their proportions repeated by each muntined pane. Window frames, baseboards, corner boards, and architrave are a single width, with a sole column supporting the porch. In a similar streamlining spirit, these lost Shingle-style Colonial Revivals viewed the ocean over the refinery at Oilport (now Sunset Palisades) with four faux *hogyo* roofs and 16 square Tuscan columns. The image below was captured in about 1930. (Above, photograph by James Papp; below, photograph by Edith Drennan Gragg.)

When, in 1889, "Major" S.B. Abbott (serial Oregon millwright, Kansas lawman, Central Coast architect, and Los Angeles oilman) designed attorney Ernest Graves's house (extant, Johnson and Palm, San Luis), the *Tribune* called it a "Romanesque cottage," presumably for the arch in its open-pediment gable. (Open pediments have a bottom gap, and broken pediments have a top gap.) The house's numerous pediments and canted and semicircular bays communicate Colonial Revival. Ridge cresting, windows with perimeter stained-glass panes, doubled square rather than Neoclassical columns, and painted shingle siding hybridize Eastlake. The 1895 Erickson House (extant at Broad and Islay Streets) uses pediment gables, a bellcast segmental entry pediment with Ionic columns, and a Colonial Revival bellcast tower roof. Then it adds a Juliet balcony with a Moorish horseshoe arch and Indo-Islamic screening—like *hogyo* roofs, cheerfully amalgamated into American Colonial Revival. (Above, photograph by L.M. Fitzhugh; below, photograph by J. Barron Wiley.)

The entrance pediment, pediment gables, and round towers of the 1889–1891 Hotel El Paso de Robles communicated Colonial Revival, but the arched windows and inset dormers were usually associated with Queen Anne or Châteauesque. The slender, towering chimneys, more suited to the East Coast than earthquake country, were a McKim, Mead, and White borrowing from British Queen Anne. The open tower tops' columns were (more or less) Tuscan but the porch columns were a bizarre mix of Italianate capitals with spindle shafts. Even more bizarre, the 1906 Arroyo Grande Union High School married a streamline Colonial Revival bungalow (pagoda roof, joined windows, Tuscan columned asymmetric entry porch) to a Mission Revival bell tower, whose Mission San Luis Rey-sourced Flemish gable with flanking pedestals, a descendant of the Baroque attic panel with segmental pediment, would end up on a thousand Taco Bells.

The Hotel El Paso de Robles used more than a million bricks in its load-bearing walls; the Hotel Ramona in San Luis, 460,000 shingles to clad its wood frame. The 1888 Ramona was named after Helen Hunt Jackson's 1884 novel. Written to address California Indians' plight, it instead supercharged California tourism. Oakland architect Walter Mathews designed the hotel's exterior in Shingle-style Queen Anne, using shingles to create curvature, in the rounded dormer on the left and the eyebrow dormer on the right. A private suite—Gertrude Jack, at left, was the hotelier's daughter—referenced Charles Eastlake, Christopher Dresser, and the Aesthetic style: an etched and spindled fireplace surrounded with exotic tiles and curio shelves, Dresserian kettle and stand, tea with eclectic china, lily-papered walls, and ladies gowned loosely. The Ramona burned in 1905, and the "fireproof" El Paso de Robles followed in 1940.

William Weeks designed this sophisticated 1906 house for LeRoy Smith, later the second director of Cal Poly, in High-Peaked Colonial Revival—a Shingle-style subset of the First Bay Tradition. High-Peaked Colonials were usually tucked into narrow Bay Area lots. Since the Smith House is at the corner of Johnson Avenue and Mill Street in San Luis, it displays its long side as a front façade with square Tuscan columns. The half-story open-pediment gable is borrowed from c. 1830 Cape Cod Greek Revivals. Though Julia Morgan modeled the Monday Club exterior on Palladio, inside she adhered to the First Bay Tradition with an exposed, Medieval-looking roof truss. Its sophisticated engineering included tension king post and compression crown posts connecting rafters to collar beam, supported in turn by arch braces. Morgan graduated in engineering at Berkeley before studying architecture in Paris. (Above, photograph by James Papp.)

Contractor Charles Strickland built extraordinary *japoniste* Colonial Revival bungalows in San Luis, including two survivors with irimoya roofs, a Japanese temple form of gable surrounded by hip. This one on Buchon's 1100 block, he built for himself in 1905: a masterpiece of crossed irimoya roofs, square Tuscan columns, and columned and canted house corners, mirrored by canted interior porch corners. Given previous experimentation with the form (Islay and Garden in 1904), it seems likely he designed it himself. Also built in 1905, on Mill's 1300 block, architect L. H. Lane's extant Page House displays not only an irimoya roof but hexagonal and heptagonal arches. A concrete foundation and an asbestos layer under the (probably originally unpainted) wall shingles were for earthquake-proofing and fireproofing. A central great hall with a fireplace for afternoon tea shows English influence. (Both photographs by James Papp.)

Seven

MISSION, ADOBE, HACIENDA, AND SPANISH REVIVALS

Helen Hunt Jackson intended the novel *Ramona* as *Uncle Tom's Cabin* for California Indians, who had lost 90 percent of their population to Spanish, Mexican, and American enslavement, massacres, and disease. Instead, it inspired mission nostalgia. The 1893 Chicago World's Fair asked state pavilions to use representative architecture; California chose missions; and A.C. Schweinfurth, Page Brown, and Bernard Maybeck invented Mission Revival: a mashup of missions with some Spanish, Moorish, and palms. (Courtesy of the Huntington Library.)

In 1903, Cal Poly turned to William Weeks for its first buildings; he turned to Mission Revival. Spain having ruled the Netherlands, Mission San Luis Rey had adopted a Flemish gable for its façade, which Schweinfurth, Brown, and Maybeck used as the California Pavilion entrance, inserting the Mudéjar star window from Carmel. Weeks strayed little from that model, though flanking towers, Juliet balconies, and arched windows are Italianate. San Luis Obispo's Milestone Mo-Tel—in 1925, the first motel so-called—was designed by Pasadena bungalow court architects Arthur and Alfred Heineman. One building's frontage on 101 is defined by a domed tower and arcade. The other building's frontage is defined by a peaked gable with Mudéjar attic vent and *espadaña* (bell gable). The flat-roofed bungalows were arguably Pueblo Revival, while the tower's draped wrought-iron Juliet balcony was Hollywood Spanish. Only the towered building and façade of the gabled building survive. (Below, photograph by Bob Plunkett, courtesy of the Huntington Library.)

Mission Revival was not just for adding historical veneer to a new institution or luring tourists from US Route 101, also known as El Camino Real. Even a 1907 oil refinery could be dignified by San Luis Rey's Flemish gable and Carmel's four-pointed, four-lobed Mudéjar star window. A utility building sported a *hogyo* roof, and a Shingle-style Colonial Revival from page 83 is visible at right, presumably worker housing. A tsunami destroyed the pier and pipeline in the first year, dooming the facility. Up the coast in 1926, at San Simeon's deepwater port, Julia Morgan designed a Mission Revival warehouse (extant) for William Randolph Hearst (with a strongroom for art treasures). Its two end gables, facing land and sea, use not just Carmel's Mudéjar star window but also the circular arch of its façade. (Below, watercolor by Alice Cushing.)

Builder-architect Egbert Delaney "E.D." Bray learned his trade from relatives who constructed Hollywood sets. He worked in Craftsman, Colonial, Lutyensesque, and Spanish Revival and also executed this remarkable 1923 Art Deco–Cubist Mission Revival, surviving on Morro near Mill in San Luis Obispo's Mill Street Historic District. Bray stylized Mission San Luis Rey's central Flemish gable and odd flanking mini-gable to low angles, with a mirror image of the central gable reflected in the porch parapet below. The Sycamore sulfur springs on the way to Avila, discovered by Dr. G.B. Nichols when he was unsuccessfully drilling for oil, went Mission probably around 1920 with the minimal three arches suggestive of an arcade and flanking Monterey Style Revival buildings, whose square-columned galleries with Roman lattice balustrades recognizably conjured early California Greek Revival. (Above, photograph by J. Barron Wiley; below, photograph by Bob Plunkett, courtesy of the Huntington Library.)

In 1936, the American Bitumuls Company mixed its road-surfacing bitumen emulsion with adobe, rendering the bricks waterproof. This sounds bizarre, but immediately after the birth of the Mission Revival (in 1893) and Pueblo and Hacienda Revivals (in 1894, with A.C. Schweinfurth's Hacienda del Oso for W.R. Hearst) came the Adobe Revival: authentic architecture through authentic material. In 1939, the Golden Gate International Exposition featured a historic adobe reproduced in bitudobe. Louis Heyd saw it and, enthralled, returned to San Luis to build the first bitudobe demonstration house at 614 Monterey Street, a Mid-Century Modern by Santa Barbara adobe architect William Scott, open for public tours. In 2023, the City of San Luis Obispo razed it to build a Mission Revival parking garage. The surviving Nelson and Garris Commercial Building (605 Santa Rosa Street) was San Luis's last-built bitudobe in 1974. (Both photographs by James Papp.)

In 1926, after the Santa Barbara Earthquake, San Francisco architect William Mooser commenced a beloved landmark, the Santa Barbara County Courthouse, in Hacienda Revival. The same year, also in Hacienda Revival, Mooser commenced San Luis Obispo's county hospital. Less opulent of design and materials, it nonetheless includes defining characteristics: a tower, cantilevered gallery, box balcony (*balcón de cajón*), projecting wrought-iron grille, and low-pitched tile-covered roofs. Though surviving, it has been encrusted by modern additions—a fate spared Santa Barbara's courthouse and this gorgeous hacienda-style house in San Simeon for the Hearst Ranch's head cowboy, designed by Julia Morgan in the 1920s. Its round observation tower, wood grilles, and chimneys with brickwork based on pointed Moorish lambrequin arches are enclosed by a scalloped wall.

Julia Morgan designed over 700 projects in her career, of which Hearst Castle was one. She would, according to architect and employee Walter Steilberg, work at her San Francisco office without break from 8:00 a.m. to 7:30 p.m., take the 8:00 p.m. train to San Luis, get a lunch-counter meal at 2:00 a.m., then make the four-hour car ride to San Simeon "to put in a full day on the job" on Saturday. She followed the same schedule on Sunday, with the night train back, nearly every weekend from 1919 to 1938. She designed not just the buildings, but also the landscape of La Cuesta Encantada. "Her designs were her own work," Steilberg wrote, down to this simple but elegant half-circular bench of three ogees overlooking the spectacular landscape. Views of and from the enchanted hill are the essence of the site.

Steilberg, who worked for nine of California's most prominent architects, called Morgan "more talented an architect than any of these able men" and "far more accomplished in the area of building technology" because of her job site presence and observation and questioning of craftsmen. Morgan first worked for Phoebe Apperson Hearst, converting Schweinfurth's Hacienda del Oso, built for the son, into a Spanish Revival château for the mother. The month Phoebe died, W.R. Hearst was in Morgan's office, asking her to design, at San Simeon, a "Jappo-Swisso bungalow," that is, a California Bungalow like the ones Greene and Greene built in Pasadena. Instead, Morgan and Hearst would collaborate on a Platersco palace (above) half-circled by three Hacienda–Spanish Renaissance Revival "cottages" (central Cottage C, below). Spanish Renaissance Plateresco—"like a silversmith"—sets off bare walls with opulent, angular Gotho-Mudéjar ornament.

California's seismic geography lends to its great architectural feature: descending hillside houses. From the 1870s to 1960s, First and Second Bay Tradition houses clung to San Francisco and East Bay hills: seeing and being seen. But the Hacienda del Oso—transformed into Phoebe's Hacienda del Pozo de Verona with tile roofs, pergolas, and the flanking towers that, the Ecole des Beaux-Arts had taught Morgan, characterized châteaus—sat on a plateau below Pleasanton's hills. Wyntoon—the Hearst camp where Maybeck built a seven-story castle for Phoebe and where Morgan built a Bavarian village for W.R. after Maybeck's castle burnt down—occupies a river hollow in Mount Shasta's shadow. La Cuesta Encantada offered the ideal hill site, towering over landscape and seascape. Morgan's descending terraces, with balustrades, balconies, belly grilles, and anthropomorphic beam ends, show the detail of Hearst and Morgan's vision. Steilberg observed Hearst's grasp of working drawings: "None of the very able architects and engineers with whom I have worked could 'translate' from two dimensions to three more quickly or more accurately."

This pre-temple version of the Neptune Pool showed Morgan's attention to landscape, as well as hardscape. Herms, urns, globe lamps, palms, and cypresses accented the water. The globes would later go on top of the herms. Hearst was not above kitsch—but always rich kitsch. The final, 345,000-gallon version did not look out of place in Lady Gaga's 2014 singing, dancing, synchronized swimming Greco-pop "G.U.Y." video. (Scandal ensued when filming required the pool to be topped up during a drought.) But Morgan was also a genius of personal spaces, like this opulent but intimate arched and coffered room. Morgan's job was to incorporate the thousands of pieces of interior architecture that Hearst's agents bought in Europe, including whole ceilings, walls, rooms, and buildings. He inherited his vast collecting sweep from Phoebe Apperson Hearst, who sponsored and went on her own archeological digs.

The Refectory is a favorite room, perhaps for the combination of Medieval splendor, Hollywood glamour, and Hearst's plebeian tastes in food. The structure features a Cinquecento (Italian 1500s) ceiling with hagiographic bas-reliefs (carved saints) framed in its coffers, Spanish Gothic 15th-century choir stalls and 14th-century wrought iron rood screen, and trefoil arches of the musicians' loft (where music was piped). Drawn by Morgan in September 1919, only five months after her patron requested a "Jappo-Swisso bungalow," the Refectory's height was insisted on by Morgan, and its clear glass was requested by Hearst. Here, light streams through the high, south-facing windows to prove both of them right. The ogees topping the Gothic arches turned up inverted in Julia Morgan's benches outside.

Craftsmen depended on Hearst and Morgan through the Great Depression. Atop the north tower, photographed from the south, the master, in shirtsleeves and a homburg hat, prepares tile while a journeyman, in newsboy cap, contemplates the view. Tiles came from Berkeley's California Faience, as art tile boomed in Bay Area and Los Angeles. The hill's main building is reinforced concrete faced with tile and stone and decorated with Medieval Spanish figures and modern cast stone ornament in seamless bricolage. The teak gable connecting the towers was serendipitous surplus from shipwrights and bought at a bargain in 1930. One of Morgan's architects considered it a "Maybeckian flourish"; Steilberg thought it too "Japonesque." By 1938, the money for flourishes had run out. Unused treasures were auctioned and retailed in department stores, and administrators took over Hearst's media empire. Hearst retired to Wyntoon during the war, returned to the castle after, and died in Beverly Hills. He left the castle to the people of California in memory not of his father, George, who dug the family's fortune from the ground, but of Phoebe Apperson Hearst, who taught him to spend it.

Eight

Prairie School, California Bungalow, Second Bay Tradition, and Usonian

The big 1914 California Bungalow at Johnson Avenue and Mill Street in San Luis, built for banking scion George Andrews—shows "Swisso" origins: broad gables, deep eaves, and knee braces. The tiny one was designed by Julia Morgan for the daughters of cabbie Steve Zegar, who drove Morgan to Hearst Castle for two decades. It moved here from Zegar's house down the hill when his daughters outgrew it and has since moved to Purple Sage Lane.

Cal Poly's second director, LeRoy Smith, sold its first director, Leroy Anderson, his neighboring lot at Johnson Avenue and Mill Street. Counterpointing Smith's High Peak Colonial, Anderson built a natural wood Prairie School—subsequently painted white with green shutters to look Colonial Revival. Though influencing late Colonials, Prairie is quite distinct: horizontal (the ridge rather than the pyramidal end of the hip roof faces the street); angular (avoiding bellcast roofs); absent of Classical references; usually symmetrical; with long rhythmic window strips, mid-wall horizontal molding, and thrusting entrance porches. San Jose architect Charles McKenzie's 1914 Barneberg House (below), 550 Dana Street, San Luis, uses Chinese openwork wall tiles for the entry porch parapet. McKenzie also designed the Prairie School Norton House, 1066 Palm Street, constructed by his sometime student E.D. Bray.

This California Bungalow, built at Rancho Atascadero just before E.G. Lewis bought the rancho for his White-only colony, became the Lewis residence, "Headquarters House." Its shady eaves, porch, and pergola were as iconic of California life as these flanking *Washingtonia filifera*. It was torched for a supermarket in the 1960s. The bungalow form originated for heat-stricken European colonists in 17th-century Bengal. Boston-born Rev. Joseph Worcester brought it to California, designing an influential wood-shingle one-story with a square-columned veranda for a Piedmont hilltop in 1876. In 1901, New York–born, Paris-trained, Berkeley-based architect Bernard Maybeck added the Swiss elements. In 1904, Ohio-born, Boston-trained, Pasadena-based architects Charles and Henry Greene melded the Swiss to Japanese (lower-pitched roofs, accentuated rafter tails, and horizontal beams and crossbeams). Architect J.C. Simms even employed the Japanese dual-pitch gable for the distinctly bungaloid 1917 Simmler School.

Fred and Mary Crossett's 1914 house, a masterpiece of *japonisme*, listed E.D. Bray as contractor as well as architect. Graduated front gables create a pagoda effect; the crossing side gable creates an *irimoya* effect. Porch crossbeams are Japanese *hari* supported on pillars and supporting perpendicular beams. Overhanging lintels evoke a *torii* gate. Dual-width clapboard and stuccoed chimneys add subtlety. Fred Crossett managed Channel Commercial (see page 75). The house still stands at Buchon and Morro in San Luis. Bray, in a suit and rakish homburg, posed with his craftsmen before Joe and Lena Wilkinson's house at Marsh and Carmel. "Designed by E.D. Bray," according to the 1914 permit application, its knee braces, sash windows, and birdsmouth rafter tails remain unchanged. Joe owned a gas station, appearing in greasy coveralls at the kitchen door for Lena's elegant bridge party guests, disappearing before she spotted him.

This interior of the George Andrews house (see page 101) shows the hallmarks of a Craftsman interior: shoulder-high wainscot, built-in glass-fronted bookcases, (faux) exposed beams, and a nook with built-in benches near the brick fireplace. In colder climates, this last would have been for warmth, but in California, it was for light and air. The contractor and possibly architect was Theodore M. Maino. Ken Schwartz's 1959 design for the Peter and Carol Andre House uses carved beam ends, board and batten, and river rock for rusticity, shed roof and floor-to-ceiling glass for modernity, enclosing huge indoor areas with spectacular views. Schwartz studied architecture at the University of Southern California (USC), but his Mid-Century Modern design relates to hillside houses to the north by architects like Joseph Esherick and Henry Hill in the Second Bay Tradition. (Above, courtesy of Minke Winklerprins, MD; below, photograph by James Papp.)

When PG&E decided to build a power plant by Morro Rock, it looked not for an engineer but an architect who could complement a natural landmark, choosing William Gladstone Merchant. Merchant started his career assisting Maybeck with the 1915 Palace of Fine Arts, a beloved Roman temple and the Panama-Pacific International Exposition's sole survivor, restored twice by Merchant. He designed the Temple of Youth and Temples of the East for the 1939 Golden Gate International Exposition and borrowed Greco-Roman temple forms for San Francisco buildings, including the recently restored PG&E Mission Substation. His two-stack design for the 1954 Morro Bay Power Plant resembled the obelisks, hall, and sanctuary of the Temple of Luxor, sheathed in glowing aluminum. Built with one stack, increased to three, it is now closed and condemned. The Bauhaus-style Atascadero State Hospital, also from 1954, survives. (Above, courtesy of the Environmental Design Archives, University of California.)

Wisconsin-born ophthalmologist Karl Kundert, encountering Frank Lloyd Wright's buildings in Madison, approached Wright in 1953 to design his office at Santa Rosa and Pacific in San Luis. "I felt I'd be spending a lot of hours working, and they might as well be in a friendly ambiance as opposed to one that is hostile," he said. Wright charged Kundert $1,500, meeting with him repeatedly in Scottsdale and San Francisco to work out a design. With double-height, clerestory-lit reception and single-height offices, it resembles Wright's "Usonian" (his word for *American*) houses, appearing to be his only Usonian office. Kundert said, "I told him I wanted to get away from the small waiting room with old magazines," hence the fireplace and creekside patio fringed by sycamores—"the people's tree," according to Wright. Now a cardiologist's office, its Wright-designed furniture is in storage, as the pieces were deemed too difficult for heart patients to get up from.

Wright conceived Organic Architecture; Warren Leopold lived it. In *Big Sur and the Oranges of Hieronymus Bosch*, Henry Miller wrote of Leopold, "His idea, or ideal, is to so manage that [his family] won't need a house—they will all live together in a tent—or under a rock. Warren loves to build houses but loathes his profession." With one child seriously ill, Leopold moved to Cambria, closer to San Luis doctors Lawrence Field and Benjamin Cox, for whom in 1967 he built this tent-like, rock-like clinic, 84 Santa Rosa, whose waiting room's lamps were made by Morro Bay's Gerald Rupp and transparent table looks through to Brizzolara Creek. One owner of a Leopold house said, "It has one right angle. You'll never find it." His buildings, scattered around the county, concentrate in Cambria. He defiantly signed himself, "Not a Licensed Architect." His family engraved it on his tombstone. (Both photographs by James Papp.)

Nine

PALLADIAN, ART DECO, LUTYENSESQUE, AND MINIMAL TRADITIONAL

Cal Poly's sophisticated 1909 Deuel Dormitory—architect unknown—combined Palladianism (keystone arch flanked by columns, low-pitched roof, and deep, bracketed eaves) with the First Bay Tradition (the brackets are [faux] beam ends supporting a soffit, a Maybeck touch). The postwar Poly planning document put this and Richard Neutra's 1939 National Youth Administration (NYA) center, a modernist triumph, on the chopping block. Only the NYA center (see page 118) would (somewhat) survive.

In 1911, two buildings in San Luis were completed based around a Diocletian or thermal window: the half-circular, tripartite window from the Thermae (public baths) of Diocletian in Rome. Palladio used the window design prominently in his Villas Pisani and Foscari and churches San Francesco della Vigna, San Giorgio Maggiore, Il Redentore, and Santa Maria della Presentazione. The Methodist Episcopal Church at Morro and Pacific used Diocletian windows prominently in its street façades. For El Monterey Theater, converted into the Obispo in 1928, the Roman latticed Diocletian window comprised the whole façade, until it was surrounded by a neon marquee. The Methodist Episcopal church was demolished in 1959 for a parking lot, now a parking structure. The Obispo burned in 1975, replaced by a mixed-use development with Diocletian windows above retail.

Atascadero was created by periodically indicted and bankrupted publisher E.G. Lewis as a utopian community—albeit a utopian community for Whites only. Palladianism was the style chosen for public buildings like the since-demolished grammar school (above right) and train station and the surviving Printery and 1918 Colony Administration Building (above left). The last is based on Palladio's four-porticoed La Rotonda (though adding a central arch to the colonnades) via the Earl of Burlington's Chiswick House (source of the dome's octagonal base) and Jefferson's Monticello (source of its hexadecagonal mezzanine's oculus windows). Julia Morgan also borrowed from La Rotonda for the Monday Club, though giving a faux cruciform appearance from the street while creating just two needed entrances, on the northwest and southwest facades toward Monterey and Andrews Streets. (Below, courtesy of Special Collections and Archives, Cal Poly San Luis Obispo.)

The 1916 Santa Margarita School (demolished) was designed by the Atascadero Colony home builders' service and built by the contractor of the Printery and Colony Administration Building, hence its appearance, the central arch and flanking entrances mimicking a Palladian window. Atascadero was legally White, and the Monday Club only functionally so, but on some occasion soon after its building opened, May Louis Watson, Ah Louis's eldest daughter, and her niece Elsie Louis showed up to be photographed in the foyer, probably for its 1934 Pageant of Nations on the historic nationalities of San Luis Obispo County. Mae perches like an aristocrat on the sofa arm; Elsie, a student at Mills College, sports the latest in city chic; while the Monday Club ladies might well have stepped out of Grant Wood's *Daughters of Revolution*. (Below, courtesy of Special Collections and Archives, Cal Poly San Luis Obispo.)

In 1929, Elsie Louis's parents and uncle, Young and Stella Louis and Roy Chan dler (a contraction of the family name Chan du ler), transformed a Monterey Street storefront into an Art Deco pavilion for the Gold Dragon restaurant. Art Deco combines simplified, usually curvaceous, sometimes Cubist Neoclassicism with material richness and botanical, zoomorphic, and anthropomorphic forms. Chinese architecture was involved from the beginning; the Société Chinoise des Arts Décoratifs à Paris exhibited at Paris's 1925 Exhibition des Arts Décoratifs, after which Art Deco is named. The Gold Dragon had five shades of gold leaf on its windows; a ceiling of coral pink, jade green, lavender, and Chinese blue on a background of silver; walls of mulberry tones and variegated blues on silver; ebony booths trimmed with jade green, gold, and Chinese red; and an 18-foot-high neon sign. The Chinese *wànzì* appears before its appropriation as the Nazi swastika.

Just after World War I, the deep-eaved, hard-angled California Bungalow was suddenly replaced in architectural publications across America with houses in European and Colonial Revival styles, with emptier walls dominating fewer, smaller windows, scarcely any exterior spaces, and no eaves at all. London architect Edwin Lutyens originated the style by rationalizing Tudor Revival with more streamlined forms (a sort of English National Revival Architecture), moving on to Queen Anne, Georgian, and even Anglo-Indian in his redesign of Delhi. A 1914 folio with 600 photographs and drawings introduced Lutyens to American architects. San Luis's elegant 1926 N.W. Sandercock House (extant) at Nipomo and Islay shows the Lutyensesque influence on Spanish Revival. The San Luis Post Office is government-issue Lutyensesque Colonial Revival, but for a coping of tiles and Mission gable above the swan-neck pediment and a Spanish baluster screen below.

Santa Maria architect Louis N. Crawford designed the Lutyensesque Laird House in 1931 on Mill's 1300 block in San Luis. High-pitched roof, faux-dormer vents, a hint of half-timbering, and windows of heavier mullions and transoms and lighter muntins embody Normandy Revival. The Anholm's 1936 Georgian Revival Muller-Noggle House was designed by Santa Monica–based Edla Muir, who, in 1919, at age 13, went to work for her high school teacher John Byers as he transformed himself into an architect (initially for Adobe Revival houses, as he could speak Spanish to Mexican crews). Muir earned her architecture license in 1934, partnering with Byers until 1941. Following war, marriage, and motherhood, Muir became America's most prominent woman Mid-Century Modernist, specializing in dramatic livability (two clients fled their Frank Lloyd Wright to commission a house from her). Hearst Castle's contractor, Stolte, did the construction. Both houses survive. (Above, photograph by J. Barron Wiley; below, photograph by James Papp.)

The 1948 Dexter Library at Cal Poly showed the move from more overt revivals to a less referential "Minimal Traditional," a term invented by Virginia McAlester for A *Field Guide to American Houses* (published in 1984). "Min Trad" is clearly not modernist, but it is not clearly anything else (nothing of the Dexter Library suggests Spanish or Italian; stucco and tile could be either or neither). The eaveless Lutyensesque spareness, rhythm, and absence of transitional exterior spaces distinguish it no longer from Craftsman now but from Mid-Century Modern, with its indoor-outdoor canopies and sliding glass. The delightful Min Trad bungalow below, one of a pair at San Luis's Buchon and Broad Streets, had vaguely referential but inoperable shutters and an abstract ogee above the door (like Julia Morgan's Hearst Castle bench tops). Sadly, fishscale shingling has since been added to the street-facing gables to falsely historicize it. The ogee is gone, but the shutters remain.

Ten

MODERN, MODERNE, MID-CENTURY MODERN, AND MIMETIC

Structural engineer Raymond Hill's 1942 Salinas Dam created Santa Margarita Lake to provide water for Camp San Luis. A hoof type with an inclined, variable radius arch cam, it is also a gorgeous piece of architecture, combining the power and streamlining of poured concrete. This photograph is from a Historic American Engineering Record (HAER) of the 1960s, which called it "a distinguished example of heroic engineering and construction under wartime conditions."

Viennese Jewish architect Richard Neutra moved to America in the early 1920s to work for Frank Lloyd Wright, following his friend, colleague, and rival, Viennese Jewish architect Rudolph Schindler. In Los Angeles, they became two of the world's most groundbreaking and influential modernists. Both published architectural theory in the 1933–1934 Oceano Dunes journal *Dune Forum*, but only Neutra designed a project here, a 1939 National Youth Administration center on the Cal Poly campus. This building, whose exterior juxtaposed rows of ground-floor and clerestory windows, as well as vertical and horizontal battens on plywood siding, has sadly been stuccoed, but its fenestration, structural forms, and warm interior of redwood and brick plains remain intact, thanks to the intervention of cultural heroes like former university architect Bob Kitamura.

Ken Schwartz, as a USC architecture student, was brought by architect Gregory Ain to Richard Neutra's house to sit at the master's feet. Schwartz taught at Cal Poly and, for decades, took his own students to Silver Lake for the same experience. He found himself teaching in Neutra's NYA building; Schwartz and colleague George Hasslein's 1958 Mount Carmel Lutheran Church shows the influence of their quarters. When the church was subsequently stuccoed, Schwartz refused ever again to drive by it. For his own 1962 house on San Luis's Buena Vista, Schwartz used vertical redwood and Neutraesque glass walls. Three generations of the Schwartz family joined in construction, as, after acquiring the hillside lot, they could barely afford the structure and could not buy curtains for a year. In California style, Schwartz's beloved cars are contained but displayed. (Courtesy of Special Collections and Archives, Cal Poly San Luis Obispo.)

Eero Saarinen's North Christian Church in Columbus, Indiana (commissioned 1959, finished posthumously 1964) influenced the vogue for tent-like, needle-spired hexagonal churches. Ken Schwartz proposed an unbuilt hexagonal addition to St. Stephen's in San Luis; in 1962, San Luis architect John Ross's design for Cambria's Santa Rosa Catholic Church commenced construction; and in 1967, St. John's Lutheran in Grover Beach published its new church's design (above) by Warren Gilbert and Associates of San Jose. It later housed First Presbyterian and is now Coastal Community. In the 1960s, the glowering concrete blocks of Brutalist architecture—surprisingly named by its practitioners rather than detractors—dominated universities and public housing, whose occupants had no choice in the matter, whether west or east of the Iron Curtain. Robert Marquis's Kennedy Library at Cal Poly was completed in 1980 as Brutalism was falling from grace.

Moderne was more of an evolution of Art Deco than a popularizing of modernism. Art Deco's Classicism became staid, even authoritarian in PWA (Public Works Administration) Moderne, the style of America's Depression-era government building projects, though not as looming, angular, and bleak as its contemporary Soviet and Fascist counterparts. Meanwhile, Streamline Moderne picked up on the aerodynamics of industrial designers like Raymond Loewy. Curving stucco, metal, glass, and neon, as well as molded and painted motion lines, made buildings look like they were about to take off and transformed 19th-century streets, like Main Street here in Cambria. Frank Wynkoop's PWA addition to the Romanesque Shandon Union High School makes the old building look ancient, though their spaces and fenestration are essentially the same.

The flagship of PWA Moderne in the county is its courthouse, designed by Los Angeles architect Percy Eisen and built in three stages from 1936 to 1941. The references of this staid, authoritarian building are stylized Roman: hip roofs, Roman lattice, aquilae (Roman spread-eagles), laurel wreaths, freestanding columns, Doric triglyphs (used in Rome as well as Greece), and (oddly) fasces (bound bundles of rods symbolizing the Roman magistrate's power but also by 1919 the symbol of Fascism). To the south, Percy's Theosophist father, Theodore Eisen, designed his last building in 1923: Halcyon's Temple of the People. It is essentially a tholos—a round Greek temple on a podium surrounded by a peripteron of Doric columns—except this circle is pointed equilaterally to become heart-shaped. In a rural setting, it hearkens to an ancient architecture and spirit.

The pink and neon Fremont, built in 1942 across Monterey Street from the county courthouse, is Greek to the latter's Roman, Streamline to its PWA, Ginger to its Fred. Architect S. Charles Lee, born Simeon Levi in Chicago, briefly studied architecture there, then moved to Los Angeles, becoming a prolific designer of movie palaces from Miami to Mexico City but mostly in California. His model was an auditorium and tower, usually revival. The Fremont is his only Greek Revival (and likely the only Greek Revival Streamline Moderne cinema in the world). In 1940, Lee had used a sail-form tower for Tower Bowl in San Diego. Here, he fluted the surface to resemble the strings of a Greek psalterion. Four Greek key patterns spread across the façade (lighting up in neon). Inside, acanthus leaves (Greek symbol of rebirth) and honeysuckle (of love) swirl across walls and ceilings in bas-relief and paint that glows in blacklight. The original carpet, also acanthine, glowed as well, sending the audience wild the first time the house lights went down and blacklights came up.

Multi-hued palmette points center the marquee, gold acanthus leaves curl around them, and red lotus blossoms hold the corners: these are the three parts of the anthemion, usually white and diminutive on Greek Revival friezes. Pink Vitruvian waves border the signs. The knowledge that architectural detail on ancient Greek temples was actually brightly painted became more widespread in the 20th century. With new neon colors and blacklight, Lee chose to restore the colors and enlarge the motifs. The streamlining of Streamline Moderne was inspired by the 1930s industrial design of ships, trains, planes, and automobiles. The fin on the now-demolished KVEC building on Mountain View at the foot of Cerro San Luis echoed the cars in its parking lot.

Shed roof, casement windows, natural board and batten walls, river rock dado, and trapezoidal wood banner characterized Mid-Century Modern in the 1954 Baywood Park Women's Club. Now Los Osos Christian Fellowship, sadly, its chimney has been lopped, the redwood walls have been painted, and the banner has been removed. Springfield Baptist Church, now St. Luke's, was built at the end of San Luis Obispo's Brook Street in 1948, gaining its tower in the late 1960s. Until 1942, Brook Street was Eto Street and half of Japantown. When its Japanese Americans were shipped to concentration camps, Japantown, the only area of San Luis that had welcomed African American residents, became its Black cultural hub. Mid-Century Modern low-pitched roof and river rock dado are set off by the oculus window, a feature of church façades from the Middle Ages on, innovatively quadrisected here by a cross. (Below, photograph by James Papp.)

Builders of San Luis's 1968 Madonna Plaza claimed it referenced the missions (more likely Mussolini's Palazzo della Civiltà Italiana in a parking lot). Presciently, in 1965, the Sauer-Adams Adobe's Alex Gough wryly editorialized a solution for downtown: demolish the Mission San Luis Obispo to build parking and then construct replica fiberglass "missionettes" at suburban shopping centers. In a similar countercultural vein, the Dunites—interwar refugees from consumerism and its discontents— scavenged huts in the Oceano Dunes. In about 1934, nudist and windfall vegan George Blais posed before "Arther the Navigator" Allman's hut. (Contemporaneously, Tiki architecture arrived in Hollywood with Don's Beachcomber restaurant.) Up the coast at Pismo, a headless dinosaur exemplified Mimetic architecture (and stop-work orders absent building permits).

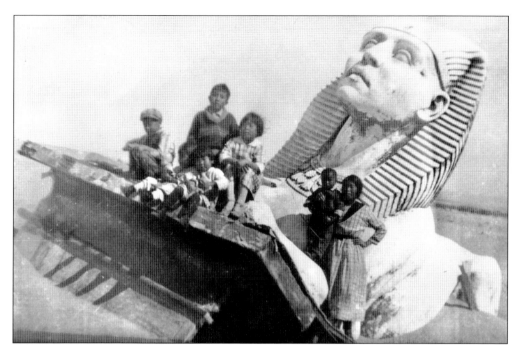

"I met a traveller from an antique land, / Who said—"Two vast and trunkless legs of stone / Stand in the desert. . . . Near them, on the sand, / Half sunk a shattered visage lies. . . . Round the decay / Of that colossal Wreck, boundless and bare / The lone and level sands stretch far away." Recalling Shelley's "Ozymandias," a Japanese American family poses on one of twenty sphinxes leading to the Gates of Rameses, abandoned after Cecil B. DeMille filmed *The Ten Commandments* in the Oceano Dunes in 1923. The Dunes Center, Guadalupe, displays excavated fragments. In Poly Canyon, students reassemble the 1957 geodesic dome built after Buckminster Fuller's 1956 Poly lecture. The first one built without Fuller's supervision, the first permanent one on the West Coast, the semi-spherical dome fulfills the nearest efficiency of materials to volume. (Below, courtesy of Special Collections and Archives, Cal Poly San Luis Obispo.)

DISCOVER THOUSANDS OF LOCAL HISTORY BOOKS
FEATURING MILLIONS OF VINTAGE IMAGES

Arcadia Publishing, the leading local history publisher in the United States, is committed to making history accessible and meaningful through publishing books that celebrate and preserve the heritage of America's people and places.

Find more books like this at
www.arcadiapublishing.com

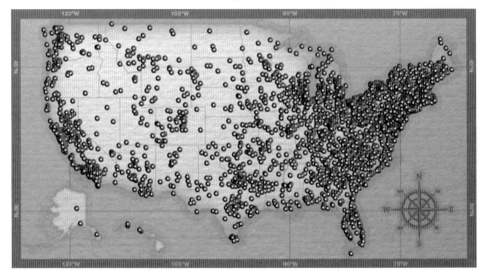

Search for your hometown history, your old stomping grounds, and even your favorite sports team.